# INSTRUMENT MAKERS TO THE WORLD
## *A History of Cooke, Troughton & Simms*

*COVER PICTURE:*
*Commencement of the total eclipse of 28 July 1851 at Bue Island, Norway. Coloured lithograph from a watercolour by Charles Piazzi Smyth, the astronomer in charge of operations. Telescopes by Cooke and by Troughton & Simms were among those used for the observations.*

# Cooke, Troughton & Simms: structure of the businesses

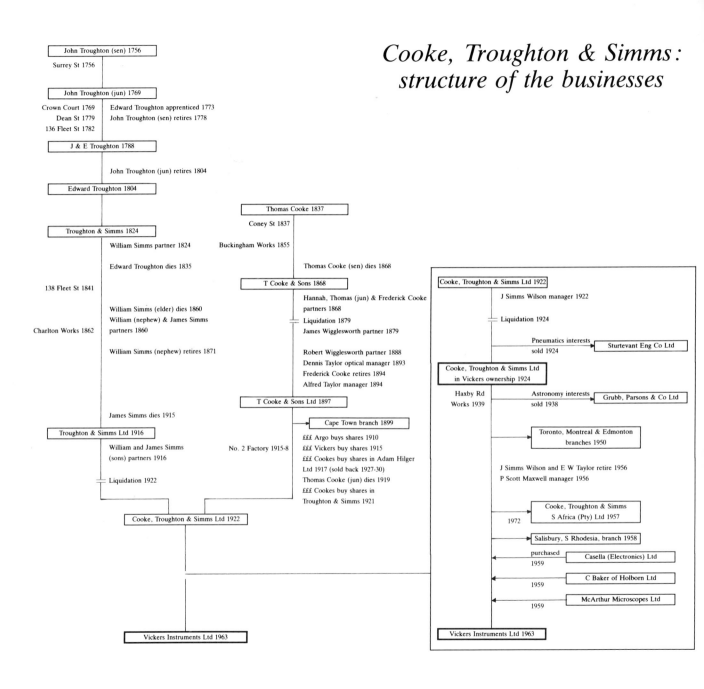

# INSTRUMENT MAKERS TO THE WORLD

## A History of Cooke, Troughton & Simms

by

Anita McConnell

William Sessions Limited
York, England

ISBN 1 85072 096 7

Printed in 10 on 11 point Times New Roman Typeface
by William Sessions Limited, The Ebor Press
York, England

# Contents

List of illustrations ... ... ... ... ... ... ... ... ... ... ... vi
Foreword ... ... ... ... ... ... ... ... ... ... ... ... viii
Preface ... ... ... ... ... ... ... ... ... ... ... ... ix
Acknowledgements ... ... ... ... ... ... ... ... ... ... ... x
Note on Terminology ... ... ... ... ... ... ... ... ... ... xi

**PROLOGUE** – THE BUSINESS OF INSTRUMENTS ... ... ... ... ... ... 1

**PART ONE – TROUGHTON AND SIMMS OF LONDON** ... ... ... ... ... 6
Chapter 1 : At the Sign of the Orrery – John & Edward Troughton ... ... ... ... 6
Chapter 2 : Master of His Craft – Edward Troughton ... ... ... ... ... 14
Chapter 3 : William Simms – From Small Beginnings ... ... ... ... ... 24
Chapter 4 : Standards of Precision – The Simms Family at Fleet Street ... ... ... ... 32
Chapter 5 : Surveying the World and the Heavens ... ... ... ... ... ... 40

**PART TWO – COOKE OF YORK** ... ... ... ... ... ... ... ... 50
Chapter 6 : The Self-Made Man – Thomas Cooke of York ... ... ... ... ... 50
Chapter 7 : Buckingham Works ... ... ... ... ... ... ... ... 57
Chapter 8 : Changing Horizons – Changing Output ... ... ... ... ... ... 69

**PART THREE – COOKE, TROUGHTON & SIMMS** ... ... ... ... ... 79
Chapter 9 : Under Vickers' Control ... ... ... ... ... ... ... ... 79
Chapter 10 : Short Focus, Wide Field ... ... ... ... ... ... ... ... 89

**EPILOGUE** – LOOKING FOR SURVIVORS ... ... ... ... ... ... ... 97

Further Reading and Notes ... ... ... ... ... ... ... ... ... 100
Index ... ... ... ... ... ... ... ... ... ... ... ... 111

# List of Illustrations

Cooke, Troughton & Simms: structure of the business ii
Lenses 3
The Troughton family 7
Protractor by John Troughton, c1785 8
John Troughton's dividing engine, c1780 9
Astronomical quadrant by J. & E. Troughton,
   Coimbra University, 1798 9
Equatorial telescope by J. & E. Troughton,
   Armagh Observatory, 1795 10
Small orrery signed 'Troughton' 11
The north side of Fleet Street, c1847 12
Fleet Street with Troughton's premises, early
   19th century 12
Edward Troughton's invoice for goods shipped
   to America, 1805 13
Edward Troughton's beam compass, 1792 15
Astronomical circle (the 'Lee circle') by
   Edward Troughton, 1793 15
Portrait of Edward Troughton 16
Huddart's equatorial telescope, 1797 17
Mural circle by Edward Troughton, Greenwich
   Observatory, 1812 18
F. R. Hassler's dedication of his book to
   Edward Troughton, 1823 19
Troughton's Fleet Street premises, 1817-22 20
The Troughton repeating circle, early 19th century 21
Transit telescope by Edward Troughton,
   Greenwich Observatory 23
The Simms family 25
William Simms (1793-1860) 26
William Simms (1817-1905) 26
Frederick William Simms (1833-1891) 26
Telescopes by Troughton & Simms and Cooke,
   Auchtertyre Observatory 27
Sir James South's telescope dismantled for sale, 1839 30
The transit circle 31

Collapse of 137 and 138 Fleet Street, 1841 33
James Simms (1828-1915) 34
Airy's Altazimuth, Greenwich Observatory, 1847 38
Patterns of theodolites 39
James Simms (1862-1939) 41
William Simms (1860-1938) 41
Latitude observations in India, c1890 41
Charlton c1877, with Troughton & Simms' Works 42
Troughton & Simms' 'water telescope',
   Greenwich Observatory, 1871 43
Standards of length by Troughton & Simms,
   Guildhall, London 44
'How summer time is recorded', Greenwich
   Observatory 44
Charlton Works, interior views, 1880-90 45
Equatorial telescope and portable observatory,
   c1872 46
Charlton Works, building a transit circle 47
Charlton Works, exterior, c1909 48
Cooke's stand at the London International
   Exhibition, 1862 49
The Cooke family 51
Thomas Cooke (1807-68) 52
Thomas Cooke (1839-1919) 52
Charles Frederick Cooke (1836-98) 52
Cooke trade cards 53
Thomas Cooke's steam carriage, c1866 54
Buckingham Works Rules and Regulations, 1865 54
Cooke's London shop, 1863-69 55
Cooke's transit for India, 1872 55
The Cooke turret clock 56
Building the Newall telescope, c1870 57
Plan of Buckingham Works, 1871 58
The Forth Bridge surveyors, 1885 59
Assembling Cookes' dome, Cape of Good
   Hope, c1896 60

Cookes' dome, Cape of Good Hope, 1896   60
Cookes' dome, Greenwich Observatory, c1892   61
Buckingham Works, interior views   63
Buckingham Works, 1906, telescope for
   Sir Thomas Sebastian Bazley   64
The Watkin Mekometer   65
Alfred Taylor (1863-1940)   65
Buckingham Works, telescope for
   Franklin-Adams, c1900   67
Cooke equatorial telescope made for Negretti
   & Zambra, c1920   68
Cooke magnetometer, 1901   70
Cooke portable transit telescope, 1904   70
Cooke theodolite for the Antarctic Expedition, 1912   71
Dennis Taylor (1861-1943)   71
Building the telescope for the Brazilian National
   Observatory, c1894   72
The Brazilian telescope in its Cooke dome,
   Rio de Janeiro   72
Cooke lens, 1908, sectioned view   73
Pollen's AC rangefinder, early 20th century   74
Cookes' women assembly workers, World War I   75
Cookes' workmen, World War II   76
Bishophill Fitting Shop No. 2, c1920   77
Watkin depression rangefinder, early 20th century   78

Surveyors on the Antarctic Expedition, 1921   78
Cooke, Troughton & Simms' offices, Broadway,
   1920-30   79
The perils of surveying, c1923   80
Diagram of the Tavistock Type II theodolite   81
Surveyors using a Tavistock theodolite   81
Cookes' advertisement for repairs, 1927   82
Vickers Projection Microscope Mk III, 1941   83
Cookes' stand at the Buenos Aires Exhibition, 1931   84
Wilfred Taylor (1891-1980)   85
Haxby Road Works, aerial view   86
Cookes' M4000 microscope, 1944   88
Cookes' long-service employees, 1912   88
Lens polishing at Haxby Road, early 1950s   90
Arthur Simms (1891-1976)   91
James Simms Wilson (1893-1976)   91
Surveying with the Tellurometer, c1960   92
Cooke-McArthur microscope, c1960   92
Francis Smith   93
Everest theodolite, 20th century form   94
Display of Cooke theodolites and levels, 1969   95
Vickers Projection Microscope, 1962   96
Cookes' Forth Bridge theodolite, 1884   97
Troughton reflecting-repeating circle   98
Cookes' dividing engine, c1868   99

## PICTURE CREDITS

# *Foreword*

COOKE, TROUGHTON & SIMMS is a name known and respected throughout the world in the field of scientific instruments. It has a history going back over 200 years to the Troughtons and then to the Simms in London, and some years later to the Cookes in York. They were all drawn to the craft of fine instrument makers by their love of hand-made precision engineering.

Anita McConnell, a well-known historical authority in this field, has now recorded in detail the fascinating story of how the business grew from small beginnings in a yard behind Fleet Street in London into a world-renowned manufacturer. She records how the parts of the business were brought together as a subsidiary company of the armaments giant, Vickers. She records, alas, the final disappearance of the famous name from the ranks of scientific instrument makers.

Anita has drawn upon her own extensive and expert knowledge, and has also delved deeply into many collections, archives and libraries. Her long list of acknowledgements reveals the extent of her research.

A collection central to the subject is the Vickers Instruments archive at the University of York. The documents and photographs are in the Borthwick Institute there, while examples of the actual products are in the Physics Department. Until a few years ago

these were all held at the works of Cooke, Troughton & Simms in Haxby Road, York; they have now been sorted, arranged and indexed by Alison Brech, thus saving them from a fate all too familiar to company historians.

It is most appropriate that the archive has been retained in York. For this we are grateful to the University authorities, particularly to Professor Jim Matthew and to Dr David Smith who have given the fullest support both to the setting up of the archive and to the writing of this book. It is to be hoped that these will encourage others to carry out futher research in the scientific, historic and economic fields covered by Anita's book.

A collection complementary to the Vickers Instrument archive is that containing the Vickers head office records now lodged with the Cambridge University Library. This covers the wide-ranging armaments and commercial activities of Vickers and its forebears, including those of the later activities of Cooke, Troughton & Simms.

We are all most grateful to Anita McConnell for recording this most interesting story of a long-established company in the field of scientific instruments.

HUGH SCROPE
Company Secretary of Vickers Limited
1967 to 1984

# *Preface*

IN 1946 SELECTED CUSTOMERS AND friends of Cooke, Troughton & Simms of York received a small book, its blue cover embossed with a gold orrery and the words 'At the Sign of the Orrery'. Subtitled 'The origins of the firm of Cooke, Troughton & Simms Ltd from material collected by E. Wilfred Taylor and J. Simms Wilson', it was privately published and distributed. In 1960 a second edition was published 'brought up to date by P. D. Scott Maxwell', who had succeeded Taylor and Simms Wilson as Managing Director. Since then, though many valuable studies of some aspect or period of its business have been published, no full history of this company has been attempted.

Taylor's curiosity about the origins of Troughton & Simms seems to have been aroused by his interest in dividing engines. Several of his technical papers were prefaced by a brief account of his firm's history as he understood it. Simms Wilson was the great-grandson of that William Simms who became partner to Edward Troughton in 1826. He had salvaged a few documents from Troughton & Simms' Charlton Works, and these, supplemented by family papers, suggested further lines of enquiry to document the early days of the business in the City of London. Unfortunately, World War Two was in full swing when they decided to carry out this research. Taylor and Simms Wilson were joint Managing Directors of a company fully engaged on war work. They were based in York, whilst the archives that would have helped their enquiries were either in London or evacuated to some safe place of storage for the duration of the war. They were not historians, and their method was to employ an antiquarian print-dealer named Moon to search for suitable material. Moon unearthed more information about those instrument makers – Worgan, Rowley and Wright – whose shop had been located in the western end of Fleet Street, hence the emphasis on

these characters in the book. He found nothing on the two John Troughtons, uncle and nephew, who consequently received scant attention. As a result of these circumstances, facts and dates were not checked, and sins of ommission and commission proliferated.

Cooke, Troughton & Simms Ltd was part of the Vickers Instruments Division of Vickers Ltd in 1988 when it was closed down as a consequence of a Vickers Group reorganisation. Since then, the name lives on only as a dormant 'shell company'. Vickers handed the surviving business documents and their small collection of instruments to the University of York, and these have now been made accessible for study. The University of York commissioned my research and writing of this book, which was generously funded by the Renaissance Trust.

Over two centuries have elapsed since the Troughtons first plied their trade in London; one-and-a-half centuries since Thomas Cooke set up in business in York. To write the full technical or business history of these firms, even supposing that supporting documentation could be found, would take years of time and travel. But it is said that Edward Troughton burnt all his papers when he took Simms into partnership, and many other records were destroyed for want of space or during moves from one factory to another. Nor have I had access to relevant material in the Hydrographic Office archives, which have been closed in recent years. So this book aims simply to supply the framework on which others can build according to their own interests. Suggestions for further reading are intended to help people without specialist knowledge of scientific instruments or background history; the notes are for enthusiasts with access to major libraries and the rich archive material in Britain.

# Acknowledgements

I HAVE DRAWN EXTENSIVELY on the Vickers Instruments archive, now being catalogued at the Borthwick Institute, and my first duty of thanks must be to Chris Webb, David Smith and their staff, for hospitality and friendly assistance over the past year as I worked through the numerous volumes and boxes. I am much obliged to Professor Jim Matthew of the Physics Department, University of York, who has been responsible for overseeing this project, for oiling the wheels and generally offering advice and guidance. My thanks also to Alan Gebbie of the Physics Department, who undertook some of the drawings and photography, and printed the old Cooke glass negatives, for this book. Jim Matthew, Alison Brech, Allen Simpson and Hugh Scrope kindly read and commented on earlier drafts of the text, and I am much obliged to them for this essential service.

It gives me pleasure to record here my thanks to the Directors and staff of the following institutions for their willing help, and in many cases for permission to draw on material in their collections: American Philosophical Society Archives, Armagh Observatory Archives, Borthwick Institute, York, British Library, Cambridge University Library, and Observatory, City of London and Greater London Record Offices, Guildhall Library, Map Room, and Manuscripts, Imperial College Archives, Institution of Civil Engineers, Gloria Clifton of Project SIMON (Scientific Instrument Making, Observations and Notes) at Imperial College, Public Record Office, India Office Library and Records, Lambeth Palace Library, Messrs Coutts & Co., Bankers, Messrs C. Hoare, Bankers, Midland Bank Group Archives, Museum of the History of Science, Oxford, Royal Astronomical Society, Royal Geographical Society, Royal Society, Royal Observatory Edinburgh Archives, Royal Greenwich Observatory Archives, Royal Society of Arts, Science Museum Library and Archives, Scott Polar Research Institute, Ransomes Collection, Reading.

On a personal level, I am grateful to Lajos Bartha, Luiz Alte da Vega, Mary Brück, Pamela Gardam, Dave Gavine, Julian Holland, Jane Insley, Martin Lunn, Chris McKay and Carole Stott. Former employees of Vickers and Vickers Instruments, Hugh Scrope, Robert Brech, Stephen Marshall, John Munro, Jack Andrews, Derek Cottam, Geoff Pannett, Alec Swales, and Eric West shared their memories of working at Cooke's and Bio-rad Micromeasurements kindly allowed me to look round the factory. Peter Hingley, Tony Simcock and Alison Morrison-Low gave moral support and assistance above and beyond the call of duty. My warmest thanks go to Alison Brech, presently in charge of the Vickers Instruments archive, without whose tremendous support and enthusiasm I should have frequently fallen into error and despondency.

To anyone engaged on historical research, true friends are those who selflessly share their knowledge of facts and sources. The huge file of letters accumulated during the writing of this book made me aware of my good fortune in this respect. May I now say to my correspondents from around the world, thankyou – for your contributions, suggestions and discussions, and keep writing. For my part, it has been an enjoyable and rewarding year.

It remains only to say that readers familiar with 'The Sign of the Orrery' will remark the disappearance of certain 'facts'. They will not meet John Worgan and John Rowley, whose link with the Troughtons is not proven. Regretfully the Danish National Archives could not confirm the statement on p27 that the King of Denmark awarded a 'special Gold Medal' to Edward Troughton. Nor was William Simms apprenticed to one Bennett. Any evidence in refutation of these points will be gratefully accepted . . . Doubtless other errors remain, for which I take the responsibility.

# A Note on Terminology

THIS STORY RUNS FROM the early 18th century to the late 20th century, during which time nations and empires emerged, shifted their boundaries, and, in some cases, vanished from the map. Who now can identify the multitude of small and not-so-small units of government that held sway through central Europe, or within the Indian sub-continent? Where I have used such terms as 'Germany' or 'India', these refer to geographical regions, rather than to any political division.

In dealing with dimensions I have retained the originals; a 12-inch sextant, for example, was made to that radius, not to 30.48 centimetres. Prices are given in their original pounds, shillings and pence, or guineas (where one guinea, £1-1-0, is £1.05 in decimal coinage).

Dating presents other problems. With the largest apparatus, several years could elapse between the order being given, the instrument being completed, then delivered (taking months rather than weeks, to reach America, India or Australia) and finally set up for use. The dates given here may, therefore, conflict with others elsewhere.

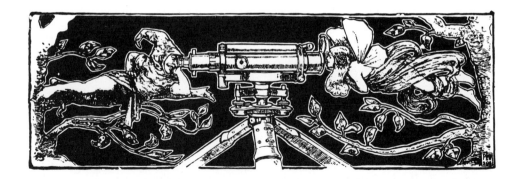

In memoriam
A. G. Thoday (1909-88)
who in 1964 introduced me to
the Troughtons . . .

# *Prologue* – The Business of Instruments

TODAY, SCIENTIFIC INSTRUMENTS RANGE from large complex astronomical telescopes to the draughtsman's accurate rulers and protractors. They include theodolites and levels, sextants and dividers, which are among the essential tools for surveying and navigation, the microscopes, balances and electrical apparatus necessary for laboratory work, and, on a more humble level, our domestic barometers and thermometers. Over the years, Cooke, Troughton and Simms and their successors made all these instruments, and many others.

The modern term 'scientific instruments' has replaced the older classification by function. Thus mathematical instruments were those with a graduated or divided arc or limb, such as sextants, sundials and rulers, whose primary function was to measure angles or distance, or to perform calculations. Optical instruments, such as telescopes and microscopes, employed lenses or mirrors to reveal what was invisible to the naked eye. Philosophical instruments, a handy catch-all term, embraced a wide variety of apparatus. There were instruments which responded to invisible forces such as magnetism or air pressure, and those which performed experiments. Magnetic compasses, barometers, static electricity machines, balances, and air-pumps all come into this group. There were models of the universe – globes and orreries – and simple teaching aids such as gyroscopes and mathematical shapes. This classification became blurred with the passage of time. Mathematical instruments such as the sextant and theodolite fitted with telescopes could sight over greater distances, and by setting magnifying lenses on their divided arcs, it was easier to read the fine graduations. Quantitative philosophical apparatus – meteorological and magnetic

instruments in particular – became more accurate and 'mathematical'. Nevertheless, during the 18th and 19th century these divisions were broadly maintained, with some instrument workshops and retailers restricting themselves to one or other class of manufacture, and craftsmen describing themselves as 'optician', 'mathematical instrument maker' or 'philosophical instrument maker'.

By the early 18th century, when our story opens, professional instrument makers could already look back on a century or so of tradition and experience. During this time they had been supplying the professional peaceable needs of land surveyors, seamen, astronomers, architects, and other craftsmen and traders. On one hand, they supplied surveying and mathematical instruments to builders of fortifications, on the other hand, they supplied gunnery instruments to help demolish them. A growing class of academics and teachers employed their calculating devices and models to explain the mathematics of earth and heavens to their pupils. Learned societies and gentlemen whose wealth matched their curiosity bought themselves telescopes, microscopes and philosophical apparatus with which to entertain themselves and their families with the study of nature. Not least, there were occasional commissions for prestige items for noble or royal collections, gifts from one monarch to another: sumptuous pieces made from ivory, rare woods and precious metals, lavishly decorated.

Although some of the larger and simpler instruments were still made of wood and iron, craftsmen made increasing use of brass and other metals as these, and the machine tools necessary to work them, became readily available. A skilled man could shape such metals to

1

closer tolerances than iron, so that the higher cost of the new metal was offset by the fact that equally good results could be obtained with smaller apparatus.

The instruments that could not be reduced in size, however, were those for measuring angles where a high degree of precision was sought. The national observatories commissioned great quadrants of six or eight feet in radius, for only on such long arcs could the instrument maker scribe fractions of a degree, enabling the astronomer to get a reading to seconds of arc. When small instruments were divided, the breadth of the engraved lines marking each degree intruded into the space between, making it difficult to estimate fractions. The art of centring an instrument and cutting uniform divisions around its circumference was generally conceded to be the most difficult, delicate and important branch of the mathematical instrument maker's craft.

The refracting telescope came into use during the early 17th century but when opticians increased the size of its object glass, or lens, they found that the image lost clarity and was fringed by a spectrum of colours. This effect is caused when white light passes through a dense material such as glass, which refracts, or bends, each wavelength to a greater or lesser degree, spreading the light into the familiar 'rainbow' of colours. When Isaac Newton (1642-1727) substituted a mirror for the lens, his 'Newtonian reflector' gave a colourless image which led to the reflecting telescope gaining in popularity. Shortly after Newton's death, a gentleman named Chester Moor Hall (1703-71) discovered that a double object glass composed of a dense flint glass concave lens and a lighter crown glass convex lens corrected the dispersed rays and yielded a near-colourless or 'achromatic' image. Hall (a barrister by profession) did not pursue his findings, and it was left to John Dollond, an optical instrument maker who learnt of Hall's discovery some years later, to patent the double lens in 1758. Dollond's patent was contested and soon other opticians were selling 'achromatic' telescopes. Glassmaking in England remained an inexact science until the early 19th century. Clear glass without bubbles or flaws was rare and usually available only in small pieces, and it was seldom possible to make lenses larger than four inches in diameter.

––––––––

For centuries man has defined his position on the earth by reference to degrees of latitude and longitude. At sea, latitude was easily calculated, even with crude wooden instruments, from measurements of the sun's noonday height. Longitude was another matter. It was known that the difference in longitude between any two places was equal to the difference in local time – for example, when it was noon at Greenwich, it was 9 am for a ship at 45°W, far out in the Atlantic Ocean. But before the invention of a marine timekeeper which could show, say, Greenwich time throughout a long voyage, seafarers were obliged to estimate their longitude by dead reckoning and many ships were wrecked in consequence. It was generally believed that it should be possible to see the night sky, and in particular the moon's track against the background of stars, as a celestial clock, for at a given hour, the moon would appear closer to a particular star as seen from Greenwich than from, say, 45°W. But before this method could be put into practice, it would be necessary to compile tables showing the position of certain bright stars for each hour of the night throughout the year, and to forecast the position of the moon for several years ahead. But the navigator still lacked some handy instrument to measure his angles with the accuracy given in the tables.

To cut a very long story short, the Royal Greenwich Observatory was founded in 1676 specifically to assist navigation, and the long task of compiling the necessary star tables began. A century passed before the first *Nautical Almanac* was published in 1767. The instruments were set up with their telescopes pointing south and within earshot of a clock beating seconds, by which the astronomers timed the exact moment that the star 'transited', or reached its highest point in the sky as it passed the southern meridian. In 1714 administration of the Observatory passed to the Board of Longitude, a government body set up to encourage and reward anyone who discovered a reliable method or apparatus

# LENSES

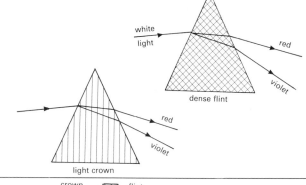

Rays of white light passing through a lens or prism are bent, or refracted, at each surface, by an amount depending on the density of the glass. Each colour making up the white light is bent through a slightly different angle, giving rise to a spectrum of colours.

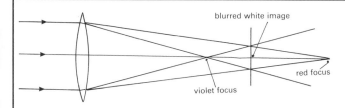

A simple biconvex lens does not bring all the colours to one focus. A blurred image is formed, and if this image is viewed through an eyepiece lens, its edges are tinged with colour.

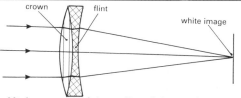

Lenses of light crown and dense flint glass may be combined to create an 'achromatic doublet', the image will be sharper, though rays passing through the lens centre may still meet at a slightly different focus to rays passing through its rim. Large lenses may still show images edged with colour.

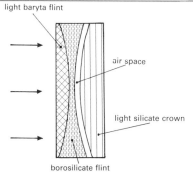

Sky photography requires a 'flat-field', with the entire field of view in equally sharp focus. It is achieved with the 'Cooke triplet', which combines three lenses with an air space. The glass composition and the radius of curvature for each lens are closely defined.

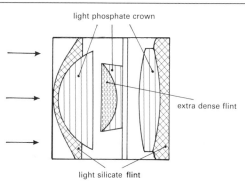

By the end of the 19th century, optical designers could specify sequences of lenses, made of different glasses and accurately figured, that eliminated most of the remaining defects and distortions.

for finding longitude. The Board also sponsored the invention of other navigation apparatus and maintained a small collection which it loaned to would-be experimenters. The Troughtons were to become closely involved with the Board of Longitude and with the Royal Greenwich Observatory.

At this time, the most promising method of finding longitude at sea was that of 'lunar distances'. For this, the navigator sighted the distance between the moon and one of the stars shown in the tables, and their respective altitudes, comparing these figures with those shown for the same hour at Greenwich. Ideally, he had to be able to measure angles to within two minutes of arc – which no wooden instrument could do. However, in 1731 the reflecting quadrant was invented, and from this evolved the brass sextant, able to measure angles of 120° with the required accuracy, and equipped with telescopic sights. When Jesse Ramsden (1735-1800) devised his 'dividing engine' which could scribe fine and regular graduations on small instruments, the Board of Longitude recognised its value and rewarded him on condition that he made details of its construction freely available. Henceforth, sextants could be made smaller, lighter and cheaper, without loss of accuracy.

---

The tools and techniques used by instrument craftsmen evolved in the workshops of clockmakers, gunsmiths and armourers, and artistic metalworkers. Hand-powered lathes and grinding machines, saws, files and abrasive powders, were available to manipulate and shape metal, and to cut screws and gear-wheels. Instrument makers had to develop for themselves the specialist arts of lens-grinding to optical standards, and the graduating of linear and circular scales. During the course of the 19th century, new metals such as platinum and iridium, new alloys such as aluminium-bronze, new materials such as rubber and ebonite, all came onto the commercial market and were welcomed into the instrument workshop, though initially with more enthusiasm than understanding. Hardened machine tools, driven at high speed by steam-engines, and then electrical power,

eventually revolutionised manufacture. Nuts and bolts and screw threads were standardised, ending the practice whereby each fastener was individually cut. It became uneconomical to subcontract work to journeymen and outworkers. The small cramped sheds and attics which had been adequate for centuries were now abandoned for purpose-built factories on the outskirts of town, where the single power source and its assemblage of machinery came under one roof, with the various specialised labour groups directed by their own foreman. Thomas Cooke, as we shall see, was a pioneer in this respect.

Besides the constraints of the available technology and materials, craftsmen laboured under various restrictions imposed by custom and practice, and by law. Under the guild system which obtained in the City of London, boys of 14 were apprenticed for seven years. Afterwards, they worked as journeymen unless or until they inherited or acquired sufficient capital to set up in business on their own account. To trade or to take apprentices, they had to become 'free' of a company, not necessarily one connected with their craft. The majority of instrument makers were to be found in the ancient Goldsmiths and Grocers Companies, or the more recent Clockmakers and Spectaclemakers Companies, both founded in the early 17th century. The Troughtons had been apprenticed in the Grocers Company and took their freedoms in it. Although the apprentice system continued, the guilds' control over traders declined in the early 19th century, as the population increased and the built-up area expanded beyond the area they controlled. Apart from this legacy of the Middle Ages, various laws, taxes and excise duties impinged upon the craftsmen. A window tax, introduced in 1696 and abolished in 1851, made adequate daylight a luxury. A tax on optical glass, not repealed until 1846, discouraged owners of glassworks from experimentation as it was levied on all glass prepared, whether marketable or not. Consequently most high-quality optical glass was imported from France and Germany. In the craftsmen's favour, at least in theory, was the patent system, conferring on the inventor of a new design or process the right to profit from his idea. Patenting was, however, both tedious and costly, until parliamentary reforms in the 1850s made it more attractive and worthwhile.

At the beginning of our period, most instruments were made to order. Personal recommendation brought orders from many European and American observatories to the Troughtons' workshop; a generation later Thomas Cooke's reputation was likewise carried throughout the United Kingdom and beyond by his satisfied customers. It was usual for leading craftsmen to have a shop where they could display examples of their range, and to have this address listed in the various trade directories that had been published from the late 18th century. Advertising played a modest part: some makers chose to have their price-lists bound into text-books on surveying or navigation, so that their names were carried outside the town where they practised. Fortunate indeed were those who received royal appointments, or, like Troughton and then Simms, and Cooke, were appointed as suppliers to one or other government agency. As the British Empire expanded, so there was increasing demand for instruments to map the new lands, to survey for roads and railways, to equip new military forces, new industries and schools. Other expanding nations with no home-grown industry sent their astronomers, surveyors and scientists to London to make substantial purchases. Promising young men were sent to work in one or other of the famous workshops, where they learnt to set up and maintain the expensive instruments that had been bought, passing these skills to their compatriots.

From the 1850s, national and international trade fairs became important showcases for the makers of scientific instruments, and brought British firms into close contact and inevitable competition with their European and American counterparts. Inside the factories, technology did not progress in isolation – workmen at their benches and clerks at their desks all had to conform to new accounting and management styles. When the going got hard, businesses that supported staff training, and research and development were better placed to survive. With a large proportion of sales exported, defective instruments could no longer be returned for repair, making it advisable to standardise on models and to produce interchangeable spare parts. More thought was given to advertising, in print and through agencies or branch offices overseas. New designs were patented abroad as well as at home. By the 20th century, German, French and American competition was eating into traditional British markets and in their struggle to survive by shifting into other products, and combining their resources, few of the long-established instrument-making firms were still controlled by the founding family. The First World War stimulated military aspects of the business but in the following slump many small businesses closed down whilst others took shelter under the umbrella of some large conglomerate which had a need for their speciality. During the Second World War production was again boosted to meet military requirements. Afterwards, the effects of dumping war surplus onto an already depressed market, coupled with drastic changes brought about by electronic technology, extinguished some survivors. Others failed to meet the high cost of research and development forced upon manufacturers who wish to keep abreast of the market. Sadly, after a long and honourable tradition stretching back more than two centuries, Cooke, Troughton & Simms has now left the field.

# Part One – Troughton and Simms of London

## Chapter 1: At the Sign of the Orrery – John & Edward Troughton

JOHN TROUGHTON SENIOR (c1716-1788) is the first member of his family known to have become an instrument maker. He was born at Corney, in Cumberland, where the family were yeoman farmers. There had been Troughtons in and around the City since before the Great Fire, and one of these may have arranged for John to come to London where, in January 1735 he was bound apprentice to Thomas Heath (c1698-1773), a leading mathematical instrument maker of the day, who worked in the Strand. His apprenticeship over, John may have continued working for Heath until 1756. In that year he was made free of the Grocers' Company, enabling him to set up in business on his own account, in nearby Surrey Street. He took five apprentices, among them his nephews, John, Joseph and Francis Troughton. In 1778 he retired from business and moved to Lewisham where he died 10 years later, leaving his estate to his widow, Catherine.

John Troughton junior (c1739-1807) completed his apprenticeship in 1764, and was still living with his uncle when he took the freedom of the City. In 1769 he married Elizabeth Davis, but she was middle-aged at the time and they had no children. John then established himself in Crown Court, off Fleet Street. Shortly thereafter he removed again, to Dean Street, Fetter Lane, where his brother Edward (c1756-1835), came south from Corney and in 1773 became his second apprentice.

At this time John Troughton was mainly employed by other craftsmen who brought their sextants and small astronomical quadrants to him for dividing. He enjoyed a high reputation in this difficult art, which was performed entirely by hand, beam compasses being used to divide and subdivide the arc into smaller and smaller segments. Whilst Edward was still an apprentice, however, John Troughton was building himself a dividing engine, based on that of Jesse Ramsden, one of the greatest craftsmen of the day. In 1776 Ramsden had received a government award for his engine, on condition that he should teach certain instrument makers nominated by the Board of Longitude how to make and use them, and it is supposed that John Troughton was one of these men. John spent three years of his spare time, plus a considerable sum of money, on this project, but it brought him enough well-paid work to enable him to acquire property outside London and, in 1782, to purchase by instalments the substantial business, with its shop and workrooms, of Benjamin Cole (1695-1766) at 136 Fleet Street, – 'At the Sign of the Orrery'. People wishing to buy fine instruments and apparatus of all descriptions had long been accustomed to call at this shop, home to a succession of eminent craftsmen, beginning with Thomas Wright (c1693-1767), who occupied it from 1718 to 1748. Wright, a former apprentice of John Rowley (c1668-1728), one of the first makers of orreries, was appointed Instrument Maker to the Prince of Wales and later to George II, and made some superb orreries in his time, which was probably why he took it as his shop sign. Benjamin Cole took over Wright's business, and is also known to have made orreries. On his death, the business passed to his son,

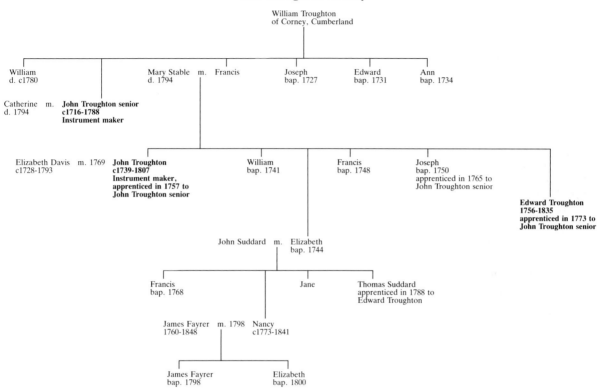

# The Troughton Family

William Troughton
of Corney, Cumberland

William
d. c1780

Catherine   m.   **John Troughton senior**
d. 1794         **c1716-1788**
                **Instrument maker**

Mary Stable   m.   Francis
d. 1794

Joseph
bap. 1727

Edward
bap. 1731

Ann
bap. 1734

Elizabeth Davis   m. 1769   **John Troughton**
c1728-1793                   **c1739-1807**
                             **Instrument maker,**
                             **apprenticed in 1757 to**
                             **John Troughton senior**

William
bap. 1741

Francis
bap. 1748

Joseph
bap. 1750
apprenticed in 1765 to
John Troughton senior

**Edward Troughton**
**1756-1835**
**apprenticed in 1773 to**
**John Troughton senior**

John Suddard   m.   Elizabeth
                    bap. 1744

Francis
bap. 1768

Jane

Thomas Suddard
apprenticed in 1788 to
Edward Troughton

James Fayrer   m. 1798   Nancy
1760-1848                c1773-1841

James Fayrer
bap. 1798

Elizabeth
bap. 1800

also named Benjamin (1725-1813), who continued to live on the premises after John Troughton took over the shop.

There was continuity of trade too, as John continued the practice of advertising in Joseph Harris' textbook *Use of the Globes and Orrery*. In the 1783 edition of that book he ran the same price list, over his own name, describing himself as 'successor to Mr Cole'. Like Cole, he bought in those items that he was not prepared to make himself. From this time, John Troughton was listed in the London Directories, which suggests that he was seeking to work more on his own behalf. From 1789 when he took his brother into partnership, until 1804 when John retired, the firm traded as John & Edward Troughton, enlarging its workshop space by taking over Cole's property in Peterborough Court. Access from this Court into Fleet Street was through a low and narrow alley, which restricted the passage of bulky items.

*Protractor by John Troughton, c1785.*

During his apprenticeship, Edward Troughton had become fascinated by his brother's dividing engine and decided to make himself a master of this art. Since John's engine was usually busy, Edward had no option but to build his own, at the same time correcting what he saw as faults on the earlier model. John's engine had a table four feet in diameter, and to divide small instruments the operator had to lean over in a painful position. Edward's dividing engine had a simpler mechanism, and being more accurately turned, he could reduce the diameter of its table. It worked at a faster rate, and the operator could cut about 24 strokes per minute without straining his back.

For instruments too large for the engine, and those where the utmost accuracy was required, Edward perfected a method of dividing by roller. This method remained Edward's trade secret until he chose to make it public in 1809. It was immensely time-consuming – he mentioned 13 eight-hour days for dividing a circle by this method, yet even this compared favourably with the previous techniques. A tapered roller, marked with divisions, was run over short sections of the limb, its marks transferred with the aid of microscopes, and these temporary marks repeatedly compared to discover and correct their errors. 'Dividing by eye' was how he described it, and certainly it demanded sharp eyesight and the steadiest of hands.

Ramsden's working life had begun during the days when fine measurements could only be made on large quadrants, either free-standing or clamped to the observatory wall. With such instruments, installed at an observatory whose latitude and longitude was accurately known, astronomers sought to measure the angular distance of stars from the zenith, this being one of the fundamental requirements of positional astronomy. Ramsden was the first to construct a large free-standing apparatus with its telescope braced within two circles, to perform the same service. The circles were six feet in diameter, carried on four vertical pillars, and the entire structure could be turned round in azimuth. It had been delivered to Giuseppe Piazzi (1746-1826), Director of

Palermo Observatory, in 1789. Edward Troughton may well have seen it under construction; certainly he heard of its subsequent performance, and when designing his own astronomical circles, he strove to avoid what he considered to be its weak points.

*John Troughton's dividing engine, c1780.*

In 1788 a consignment of large astronomical apparatus that had been commissioned from the best London makers was despatched to Portugal to furnish the new Observatory of Coimbra University. The agent for these purchases was J. H. Magellan (to give his name in the English form) (1723-90) who was demonstrator to the Royal Society. Between 1784 and 1788 Magellan made eight progress payments to Troughton, totalling £600, this being the custom when commissioning large items whose construction took years rather than weeks. The

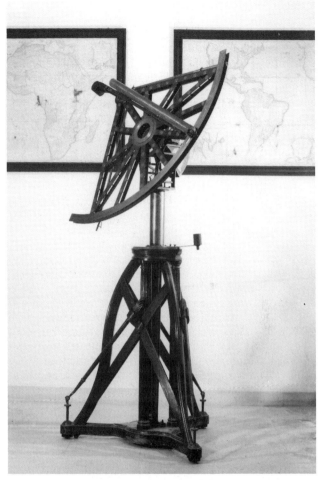

*Astronomical quadrant by J. & E. Troughton, Coimbra University, 1798.*

Troughton workshops contributed a telescope supported on a universal equatorial mounting of impressive complexity. Admired as it was before shipment, we know nothing of its performance in the observatory, for it was put into store soon after it arrived and was never put to the test. In contrast to this unwieldy item, the

Troughtons received 300 guineas for a standing three-foot quadrant ordered in 1781 and sent to Coimbra by 1798. Faced with the problem of building a substantial instrument that would not sag under its own weight, Edward had conceived the method of 'pillar construction', which he patented in 1788. The quadrant was framed by parallel flat bars, connected by small pillars. Less brass was needed, making the instrument both lighter – hence not liable to deform – and cheaper. This construction was a happy inspiration, particularly useful for small hand-held instruments, notably the 'pillar sextant'.

At about this time, Edward and John began work on a large equatorial telescope for Armagh Observatory in Ireland, founded in 1790. This may well have been Edward's first design for a telescope on a fixed mounting. Progress was delayed, first by difficulties in obtaining the necessary brass from the Angelsey Brassworks, then from shortage of manpower, coupled with a full order book. Thus it was December 1795 when the telescope finally arrived at the Observatory. Unfortunately, during an earlier sudden cold spell, the moist acid city air had condensed on its surface and had begun to corrode the brasswork. Edward Troughton later commented that it had also suffered 'some derangement of figure' though it is unclear if this was on the journey or earlier. At any rate, James Hamilton, the astronomer at Armagh, spent many months trying to adjust it to his satisfaction.

Orders flowed into the Troughtons' workshop in response to their growing reputation. Their work for the Board of Longitude was admired by those astronomers and navigators who had influence over government contracts to supply the Royal Navy, the Board of Ordnance (who were responsible for the developing national surveys), and the Greenwich Royal Observatory (of which much more later). The Honourable East India Company, with its own army and navy, and its surveyors, also knew the value of Troughton instruments. Owing to the hazards of shipping and long-distance transport, these fetched more or less their weight in gold in the sub-continent. Instruments were procured for the

*Equatorial telescope by J. & E. Troughton, Armagh Observatory, 1795.*

Company's Observatory in Madras, which opened in 1792, and any officer on home leave was sure to be asked to call at 'The Sign of the Orrery' and put a down-payment on some sextant or theodolite for a colleague back in India, for at this period the surveyors had to provide their own instruments, for which they received an allowance.

Overseas, the Troughtons came to be recognised informally as Ramsden's successors, for their instruments were bought by many diplomats and foreign visitors who carried them back to Europe and showed them off, effectively acting as unpaid salesmen. Sextants of six to 12 inches radius were in greatest demand, but occasionally orders for larger items arrived. Thus in 1793 Edward had made an astronomical circle of two feet radius for Count H. M. von Brühl, a German diplomat then living at Harefield. Von Brühl was delighted with this instrument. Edward had adopted General Roy's idea of setting microscopes over the verniers, enhancing the precision with which readings could be taken; in all other respects, said von Brühl, the circle was Troughton's own design and bore the stamp of originality and exquisite workmanship.

The same year, Edward finished a similar circle for Gavin Lowe (c1743-1815), which was hailed by many as an outstanding example of his art. This circle, also two feet in diameter, had two sets of graduations: one by lines on brass, for approximate reading, the other by dots on an inlaid gold band, subdivided to seconds by two horizontal microscopes. Lowe paid £120 for it. In 1807 this circle was sold to the Hon. Charles Greville, thence to the Rev. Lewis Evans from whom it was bought by John Lee, who gave it to the Royal Astronomical Society. A superb astronomical transit circle (that is, a circle which allows the telescope to be turned through 360°) was built for Stephen Groombridge in 1806, the only example of this kind made by the Troughtons. It was sold to Sir James South in 1823; he had four extra microscopes fitted, and continued to use it.

Edward Troughton's own design for a hand-held reflecting circle was also immediately successful. It was a modification of the portable repeating circle developed by Borda in France prior to 1787, an instrument which like the sextant was often used for finding longitude. Troughton and other craftsmen had made many Borda circles, chiefly to foreign orders, and this led him in 1794

*Small orrery signed 'Troughton'.*

to see if he could correct its inaccuracy and inconvenience. Two years later he announced his 'British Circle', which was soon better known as 'Troughton's circle'. He had dispensed with the repeating principle, confident that it was not necessary if the circle was well-divided. It was handled in the same manner as Borda's, but was built on a simpler and firmer frame, and gave more precise results. Troughton sold 200 of these circles within 20 years of its first appearance in 1796.

When newly-designed instruments were to be tested, they were carried up to a small observatory which, around 1780, the Troughtons had constructed atop their house. The instrument under test rested on a stone slab set on beams running between the party walls, whilst the standing was a floor hung on iron rods from the roof. In this way an observer could walk round the instrument

*The north side of Fleet Street, c1847, when Troughton & Simms occupied No. 138. Elevation from J. Tallis,* Views of London, *(c1847).*

without shaking it. A revolving copper dome covered the observatory. In those days, there was a virtually uninterrupted view of the meridian from north to south, and there was even a handy northern mark in the shape of a chink in the distant masonry of the church of St Andrew, Holborn. From this rooftop vantage point Edward observed and timed the transit of Mercury across the Sun's disc in May 1799, and his report was duly published with others in the astronomical literature of the day.

———

Clearly, John and Edward did not personally make every instrument that they signed. Besides meeting demands for items in common use, they were asked to turn other people's ideas into practical form. Graeme Spence's station pointer and Wollaston's dip sector came

off the drawing-board, so to speak, in this period, and there was always a backlog of old instruments awaiting cleaning and repair. Edward took his nephew Thomas Suddard as apprentice in 1788, and Joseph Dalloway in 1789. These lads worked under his eye, but in addition the brothers followed the usual practice of hiring journeymen with particular skills in one or other aspect of the trade, or possessors of some particular piece of machinery and such men might work from their own homes or alongside the Troughtons. Thus the glass lenses for Troughton telescopes came from Dollond or Tulley, both leading opticians of the time. There are records of payments made to other reputable makers, including J. & S. Brockbank, horological instrument makers; William Bardin, a noted globe-maker who lived just across the road to the Troughtons, William Gilbert

*Fleet Street, locating Nos. 136-8 and Peterborough Court, early 19th century. From Horwood's map of London, 1799-1811.*

and John Berge. Prestige was not always a safeguard against poaching and in 1800 two of Troughton's best men were lured away by the offer of higher wages.

A gearwheel cutting-engine which John Troughton had divided for his neighbour, the machinist Samuel Rehe (or Ray), and then bought from him for the considerable sum of £350, went first to a kinsman, who died in 1790, and then to James Fayrer, a clockmaker by trade and married to the Troughton's niece Nancy Suddard. Fayrer made instruments under his own name but he, and later his son, also worked extensively for the Troughtons. John and Elizabeth Troughton, his brother Edward, and Thomas Suddard, shared the house over 'The Sign of the Orrery' and when Elizabeth died in 1793, another niece, Jane Suddard, stepped in as housekeeper.

Besides their work at the bench or the dividing-engine, John and Edward had other aspects of business to contend with. Brass and other materials had to be bought in, and this required a considerable outlay of capital. On large jobs, progress payments could be demanded as work proceeded, but workmen and small suppliers had to be paid regularly, likewise the rent and the various parish rates. John built up a substantial bank balance and kept himself in credit, a situation helped by winning £270 on the government lottery in 1795.

To us John Troughton is a shadowy figure, eclipsed by his brother's fame, but there is no doubt that his contemporaries thought highly of him. When the Society of Civil Engineers was reorganised in 1793, it was decided to form a new class of honorary members drawn from craftsmen who served the civil engineering profession. Two instrument makers were to be included, and invitations were sent to Ramsden and John Troughton. Both men accepted the honour; Ramsden's illness prevented him from attending regularly but John Troughton's presence at meetings is noted on one or more occasions each year up to 1803.

John Troughton died 'of palsy' at the age of 69 and was buried at St Bride's, Fleet Street, on 28 March 1807. From an estate valued at under £3,500 he left bequests to various members of his family, in London and in Corney, with Edward as the residuary legatee. But Edward's most valuable inheritance was the sound training that he had received as John's apprentice; a training that was to bring him fame and fortune far beyond those reached by his uncle and brother.

*Edward Troughton's invoice for goods shipped to America, 1805. From archives of the American Philosophical Society.*

# Chapter 2: Master of His Craft – Edward Troughton

EDWARD TROUGHTON WAS AT THE peak of his career when John died in 1807. His new bill-heads and trade cards no longer advertised him as 'successor to Benjamin Cole'. The £400 that he inherited from his brother was a trifle in comparison with his annual turnover which, with many of his larger pieces priced between £200 and £400, probably exceeded £1,000. In the early years of the century several Troughton astronomical circles were shipped off to Hamburg, the first stage of journeys leading to the observatories of Leipzig, Gotha, Dorpat and St Petersburg. Such long-distance transport was a hazardous business. On one occasion the consignment languished in a Baltic port, delayed by the end of some local war, on another, the box containing the Leipzig circle fell off its cart along the way, and Edward acknowledged that he should have packed it into a stouter case. Besides expressing satisfaction with their costly purchases, astronomers frequently praised the excellence of their personal smaller Troughton sextants and circles. These minor instruments had usually been bought on visits to London, and it was customary for returning travellers to inform the editors of astronomical journals of the current prices there. Thus in 1800 we learn that a Troughton astronomical circle of 18 inches diameter, on a stand, cost 90 guineas; with a circle of 24 inches, 150 guineas. With the addition of a large azimuth circle and transit axis, like the one that Troughton had made for von Brühl, the price rose to 200 guineas. The largest version, with a vertical circle of 36 inches diameter, transit axis, and a telescope of 44 inches focal length and 2¾ inches aperture, cost 300 guineas. In 1802

it was reported that eight-inch 'best quality' sextants cost 15 guineas from Berge, who was Ramsden's successor, but 16 guineas from Troughton.

Besides astronomical and surveying instruments, Troughton continued to supply a wide range of mathematical instruments, increasingly needed by surveyors, draughtsmen and engineers. Any maker of precision instruments, even those based on the divided circle, needs a standard of length from which to derive his fundamental measurements. In the late 18th century, the Exchequer held sundry British standards of weight, measure and capacity, some of which deserved respect more for their antiquity than for their quality. Since no two standard yards were identical in length, it seemed a good idea to find some independent and unchanging measure, to which the yard could be related. This research was encouraged by the Royal Society and pursued by a number of scientifically-minded and suitably wealthy gentlemen, who then called on the most reputable instrument makers to provide them with delicate balances, weights and measures of capacity and of length, for the purposes of experiment. Edward Troughton made at least five standards of length, together with the necessary microscopes to compare them with other bars. The first, completed around 1792, was his own. A second went to Sir George Shuckburgh in 1796, together with a balance for weighing up to 6 lbs, a third went to the Aberdeen City authorities around 1800 (at a cost of £93-3-0). A fourth was for the visiting Swiss scientist Marc Auguste Pictet (1752-1825), who arrived in London in 1801, deposited his order with

*Edward Troughton's own beam compass and standard of length, 1792.*

Troughton, and went off to tour these islands whilst it was being made. From his own standard, Troughton prepared an 82-inch bar for Hassler in 1814-15 (as mentioned below), and towards the end of his life, probably under Simms' hand, the firm made standards for the Board of Ordnance surveys, the Danish Government and for the Royal Astronomical Society.

One of the activities which caught Pictet's eye when he came into Troughton's workshop was the art of setting a diaphragm or cross of spiders' web threads into the focus of telescopes, to aid accurate measurement. Fine-drawn silver wire had been used for this purpose for many years, but spider's filaments were finer – down to $\frac{1}{8,000}$ of an inch – and had the additional advantage of being slightly elastic and thus less liable to snap. Pictet reported how the filament was handled, and intended to make the practice known when he returned to Geneva. Edward Troughton has sometimes been credited as the first to use spider's web, but he himself, writing on the subject in 1800, acknowledged the Italian Felice Fontana as its originator. Fontana was in charge of the philosophical instruments belonging to the Duke of Tuscany. He had come to London in 1775 to commission instruments from Ramsden and Sisson, and Troughton may well have heard of the advantages of this natural filament from the man himself. Before the appearance of journals which carried such gossip, news of apparatus, methods and new materials, even something as insubstantial as a spider's web, was carried in person or by correspondence, round Europe, America and beyond.

The flow of orders into Troughton's shop must have been welcomed by the secondary trade in London, but we can name only a few of those craftsmen who laboured to his instructions. His chief assistant from about 1800 to 1817 was Josiah Dancer (1779-1835) who was involved with many of Troughton's new inventions. James Fayrer

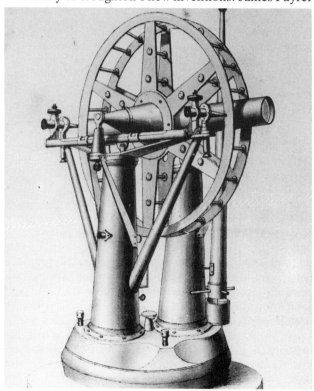

*Astronomical circle made by Edward Troughton for Gavin Lowe in 1793, it was later known as 'The Lee Circle'. From MHS Oxford, MS Gunther.*

15

*Portrait of Edward Troughton, pencil sketch by Chantry, 1820.*

their own premises in Pentonville, where they kept the second Troughton dividing engine. Henry Barrow (1790-1870), worked as a journeyman for Troughton and other leading names, and they recommended him to George Everest (1790-1866) who employed him in India for a short time. Andrew Yeates (1800-1876), born in Dublin and one of a thriving family of instrument makers, joined Troughton in 1821 and stayed for some years before moving on to become assistant at Greenwich Observatory. Robert Lawrence worked at Fleet Street for Troughton during the mid 1830s. There were journeymen from further afield – the Drechslers from Hanover, father and son, had been in London for some years. Georg, the elder, was five years with Ramsden, and his son worked for several years with the Troughtons, leaving around 1805 for the Observatory at Palermo. By the 1820s Edward was employing William Simms, whom, as we shall see, he eventually took into partnership.

———

By observations made with his own medium-sized Troughton astronomical circle, John Pond (1767-1836) had shown how inaccurate the now antiquated instruments at Greenwich Observatory had become. In 1807 Nevil Maskelyne, then Astronomer Royal, persuaded his Board of Visitors that the Royal Observatory deserved better. The first idea was to install a large freestanding circle, similar to the Palermo instrument. However, when Edward Troughton was consulted, he went home and wrote a long paper, describing a 'mural circle', a new design that he had had in mind since 1806, and setting down his thoughts about the construction and performance of the various types of circle then in use.

This document reveals a good deal about Troughton's capabilities and status at this time. For the great observatory instruments were not simply scaled-up versions of smaller portable ones, which would have been impossibly heavy and extremely costly. Their frames were lightened by the judicious use of hollow

was still active, and was joined by his son James junior, a lad whose skill and inventiveness, in Troughton's opinion, exceeded those of his father. But in 1820 Troughton recommended James Fayrer junior for the post of assistant and mechanic at the government's new Cape of Good Hope Observatory, thereby losing his services. To make matters worse, the young man did not live up to his uncle's expectations, and was soon dismissed for laziness, insolence and drunkenness. He later set up in South Africa as a watchmaker, advertising that he had worked for Edward Troughton, which shows how far afield the name earned respect. The Fayrers had

cones or trellis-work, and the axis was spring-loaded to relieve weight on the pivots. But these precautions were not enough, for unless the bearings were cast from the correct steel and bell-metal, uneven wear would quickly result. Troughton emerges from the pages of his document as a man thoroughly at home with his subject, fully aware of the possibilities and limitations of previous designs, knowing what materials and engineering strategies will suit his purpose. His well-reasoned discussion is nicely calculated to carry his official readers through to the conclusions with which he presents them.

*The equatorial telescope made by Joseph Huddart, with lens by Dollond and brasswork and divided circles by John and Edward Troughton, 1797. This unusual piece was made from tinned iron plate and was both light in weight and extremely steady in its movements. The upper circle was four feet in diameter. It, and the smaller circle at the lower end of the polar axis, were originally divided on brass. When Sir James South bought the telescope, its lower circle had become corroded and Edward Troughton redivided it on a platina band. Despite the bizarre appearance of the casing, the mounting itself was excellent, and South asked Troughton to replicate it to a larger scale when he acquired a lens of 11¾ inches in 1829.*

The proposed mural circle would turn on a stub axle set into a wall aligned north-south, so that its telescope would observe stars passing through the meridian. When the dome was opened during the day, there would be no upper frame to heat up and become distorted – one source of trouble at Palermo and Armagh. Nor would its observations depend on a plumb-line, itself a possible source of error. The Board of Visitors, at first doubtful that this entirely novel apparatus would serve the Astronomer Royal better than a conventional circle, considered his arguments and examined the model put before them (a two-feet circle which Troughton had made for Sir Thomas Makdougall Brisbane), and decided on a mural circle six feet in diameter to Troughton's design. The order was eventually given in 1809. The circle perimeters and other large parts were cast and turned at the Bermondsey engineering works of Bryan Donkin (1768-1855). Dollond supplied the lens. The circle was in place by 1811, and observations began the following year. Troughton's charge was £737, which probably included Donkin's contribution but not the cost of the lens or the masonry work supporting the axle.

This mural circle possessed another novel feature, for one of its circles was divided on an inlaid gold-palladium alloy band, the other on a platinum band. Before these metals became commercially available, the finest, smoothest divisions were those cut on inlaid bands of silver or gold, an optional extra for customers who could afford something better than brass. But silver tarnished and regular cleaning soon wore away the

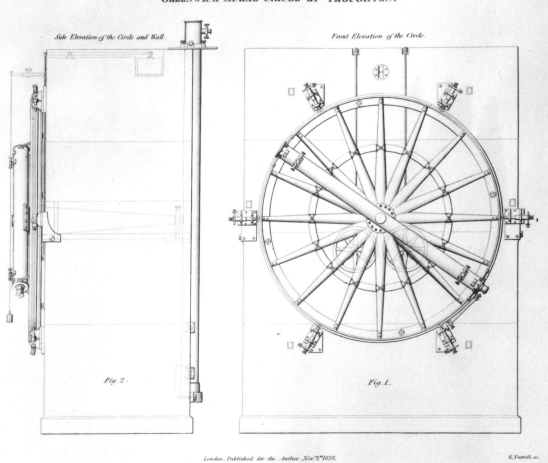

Side Elevation of the Circle and Wall.

Front Elevation of the Circle.

Fig. 2.

Fig. 1.

London, Published for the Author, Nov.r T. 1825.

E. Turrell. sc.

*The first mural circle, made by Edward Troughton for Greenwich Observatory, 1812.*

divisions and although gold remained bright, it was far more costly. By 1804 the chemist William Hyde Wollaston had discovered how to refine and produce malleable platinum and from 1806 he was supplying it in small quantities to Edward Troughton, for sextant scales. Platinum was harder than both silver and gold, it did not tarnish, and its price fell between those two metals so it was affordable and good value. Platinum-brass alloys had been tried out in telescope mirrors in the late 18th century, but Troughton is believed to have been

18

the first to cut scales on inset platinum strips on his instruments, a practice soon adopted by other makers.

---

Whilst the mural circle was taking shape, Edward Troughton sent Maskelyne a description of his methods of dividing, which was read to the Royal Society and subsequently published in the Society's *Philosophical Transactions*. His covering letter made it clear that he saw his disclosure as a valuable present to up-and-coming young craftsmen. His audience agreed. In gratitude for this generous action, Edward Troughton was elected a Fellow of the Royal Society in 1810, and was awarded its Copley Medal. This was only the most prestigious of the honours that came his way; in the same year he took up his late brother's seat as honorary member of the Society of Civil Engineers, reformed in 1823 as the Institution of Civil Engineers. In 1817 he was elected to the American Philosophical Society, and in 1822 to the Royal Society of Edinburgh. In 1823 he was presented with the Freedom and Livery of the Worshipful Company of Clockmakers. When the Astronomical Society was founded in 1820, he was among its first members, serving on its council from the first meeting, and as Vice-President in 1830-31. He was also a member of the Astronomical Dining Club which he attended regularly, and was welcomed to the houses of the astronomers who were his customers. One of these astronomers, William Pearson (1767-1847), dedicated his two-volume treatise *Introduction to practical astronomy* (1829) to Edward Troughton. He was at ease abroad, too. In 1824, he spent three weeks in Paris – 'perhaps the last frolic of my life' and saw, as he engagingly put it, 'many wise men of the South-east'.

---

In 1812 the Swiss-American surveyor Ferdinand Hassler (1770-1843) was sent to London to buy instruments for the United States' proposed Coast Survey, and although Troughton was engaged on apparatus for Greenwich, he agreed to meet Hassler's substantial order. Hassler (whose Swiss surveys had been made with

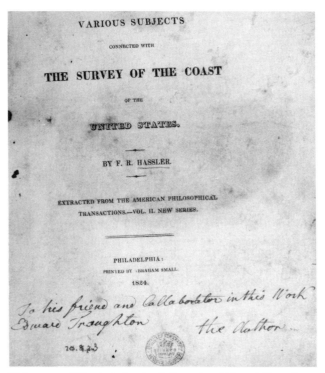

*Title page of Hassler's book, dedicated to Edward Troughton, 1823.*

Ramsden theodolites) unrolled before Troughton his own somewhat fanciful plans for a two-feet theodolite and a repeating and reflecting circle which, prudently, he allowed Troughton to simplify to more practical forms. Hassler, and his wife, moved in next door to Troughton, in order to press the urgency of his needs. Their son, born in the summer of 1813, was christened Edward Troughton Hassler in the church of St Bride opposite 'The Sign of the Orrery'. After delays caused by Troughton's illness, Hassler took back with him in 1815 three theodolites, eight circles, two transits, a telescope, barometers, thermometers, a baseline set, a balance, and an 82-inch brass scale, divided on silver, with microscope and comparator. This standard was to take its place in the United States Bureau of Weights and Measures. It was Hassler who supported Troughton's election to the American Philosophical Society. By this time there were already a number of Troughton astronomical instruments in American hands.

During the first quarter of the 19th century, there were improved 'Troughton' versions of many instruments – though not everything that he touched turned to gold, commercially speaking. Clocks, and clock pendulums, had long interested him, and he was one of the 'experts' whose opinion was sought on the rival claims of two London chronometer makers, but his own compensating pendulum, which he published in 1804, did not meet with success. His 'nautical top' intended as a marine artificial horizon, got a bad press from Captain John Ross, to whom it had been issued for trial on the Arctic Expedition of 1818. The top was set spinning by a set of wheels, like a child's toy, the intention being that its glass surface would hold steady against the ship's motion for a few minutes, whilst the observation was made. Troughton tinkered with it over the years, but had more success with his common horizon, made of black glass and levelled by a bubble laid on the surface. It was demonstrably handier in the open air than the customary dish-of-mercury level.

Troughton also turned his attention to portable barometers, as employed by surveyors to measure height above sea level. He devised a quick and effective means of resetting the mercury level when the barometer was unpacked and set up after a journey. This idea had been put into practice from 1785 and must have met with success as 'Travelling barometers to Troughton's pattern' were advertised in the catalogue of Pistor of Berlin in 1814. There was also a Troughton marine barometer, designed to hold steady in its gimbals against the ship's movement. Around 1805 he designed the Troughton level, rearranging the standard components of telescope, bubble tube and compass into a stable and really practical form. Surveyors found this level much to their liking and it enjoyed a long production life. Many of these inventions were described and illustrated in Rees'

*Cyclopedia* and in the *Edinburgh Encyclopedia*, both published during the early 19th century.

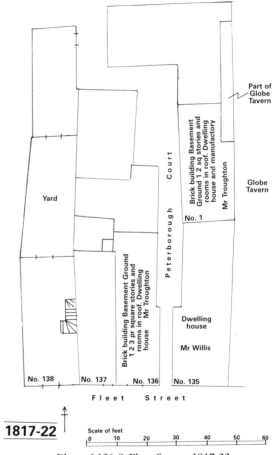

*Plan of 136-8 Fleet Street, 1817-22.*

Nevil Maskelyne died in 1811 before he could make use of the newly-installed mural circle and John Pond replaced him as Astronomer Royal. During Pond's tenure, which lasted through the remainder of Edward's lifetime, Greenwich was furnished with the major new instruments which supplied observations for definitive star catalogues. The orders did not end there, of course, for continual repairs and adjustments were called for, both on the new instruments as they settled down, and on those ancient and somewhat worn items made by the famous craftsmen of former days, which still made the occasional contribution to the Greenwich observations. However, there was the odd miscalculation, either in design or in construction, even with the Royal Observatory's instruments. Troughton's 9½-feet zenith sector of 1812 was one such. It had an illuminated plumb-line passing through the centre of the telescope tube, intended to be seen at the same time as a star was sighted, and the angular distance between them measured by microscope, but in practice both the illumination and the microscope were defective.

On the other hand, the transit telescope ordered in 1813 performed admirably. It had in fact been Edward Troughton's idea to make use of an old five-inch object glass, the largest lens ever prepared by Peter Dollond, back in 1793. He sold the idea to the Astronomer Royal on the grounds that 'the employment of this lens would mark out the dimensions of a transit instrument that would be a notable appendage to our national astronomical establishment'. The idea could not be carried to fruition until he had solved the engineering problem of preventing the great telescope from bending under its own weight. His answer was to set six tension-bars within the tubing to supply the necessary rigidity, and to fit additional external braces to support the telescope when it was not pointing directly upwards. The axis swung on pivots of bell-metal, changed to steel in 1825. Troughton's prophecy was confirmed. As mounted in the Transit Room, this telescope defined the Greenwich Meridian from 1816 until 1850. Troughton obviously thought that it did him credit, for he added a plate, dedicating this telescope and his mural circle, to the President and Council of the Royal Society.

These great instruments incorporated castings made and turned by specialist engineers to Troughton's specifications. Bryan Donkin and his son were enthusiastic

*The Troughton repeating circle, early 19th century, from Rees'* Encyclopedia, *1818, Astronomical Insts., Plate VII.*

astronomers in their own right and they collaborated in the design, manufacture and assembly of the large instruments since the Troughton premises at Fleet Street and Peterborough Court were small and difficult of access. We shall continue to meet the Donkins in later years.

In 1819 the Greenwich Observatory Board of Visitors recommended that Troughton should supply a new sector. The order was placed in 1820 but considerable delays occurred before it was erected in 1831, by which time Troughton had taken Simms into partnership and we may suppose that the latter directed its construction. The Board of Longitude was wound up in 1828, its purpose achieved. But before this door closed for Edward Troughton, another had opened: that of supplier to the Board of Ordnance, then engaged on the trigonometrical surveys of Britain and Ireland.

John Troughton, and probably his uncle before him, had supplied the professional land-surveyors with the measuring rods and chains, plane tables, magnetic compasses and simple theodolites that satisfied their requirements for preparing estate, parish and even county maps. It was the Highland campaigns of the 1740s that brought home to government just how uneven in quality and coverage were the private maps then available. It was eventually agreed that a national survey on trigonometrical principles was needed, taking into account the curvature of the earth, so that the entire British Isles could be mapped without undue distortion. This required first, the setting-out of a carefully-measured baseline, its latitude and longitude fixed by astronomical observations. Then, starting from the ends of this base-line, a network of bearings would be carried from one mountain-top to another, the length and breadth of the kingdom, providing a geographical frame within which local surveyors could map detail by their accustomed methods.

This infant survey which had been coaxed into life under the guidance of General William Roy (1726-1790) passed at his death into the charge of the Board of Ordnance. By that date, some basic triangulation had been laid down in southern England and connected with the French network, so that the latitudes and longitudes of the national observatories of Paris and Greenwich were no longer disputed. Ramsden had constructed the great theodolites and the base-measuring rods on which the survey depended. During Troughton's involvement with it, the Ordnance Survey was directed first by William Mudge (1762-1820), and then by Thomas Colby (1784-1852). By 1825 the British triangulation was nearly complete and the field of operations moved to Ireland. Colby, and his assistant Thomas Drummond (1797-1840) became regular visitors to Fleet Street, which was no great distance from the Survey's Headquarters in the Tower of London.

As mentioned above, Troughton instruments were highly sought-after in India, where officers engaged in revenue and topographical surveys praised their excellent design and reliability. There was lively competition for all second-hand Troughton instruments. In 1815 Indian officers were told that the price in London of a new theodolite was 53 guineas, that of a sextant, 40 guineas. And to this would be added the cost of shipping and overland transport within India, plus insurance – essential, given the likelihood of piracy or theft en route. After about 1820, the East India Company itself paid for those instruments requested by the governors of its Presidencies, which were issued for use in the field as required. The Company appointed William Gilbert of Leadenhall Street in London as their supplier, but this appointment was not exclusive and Troughton continued to supply instruments to them. Indeed, it was at this time, and according to some sources, in connection with work for the East India Company, that William Simms comes into the picture.

Edward Troughton was by now widely known and respected. The total value of the major items that he made for Greenwich Observatory and other government institutions in Britain and abroad must have been substantial. He enjoyed a wide market in northern Europe, which by the time of his death Britain was beginning to lose to the developing German optical industry. No stuffed shirt, he was a quiet and modest man. He possessed a comprehensive library, and when the weather permitted, enjoyed nothing better than to go fishing or walking in the country.

*Transit telescope by Edward Troughton, 1816, Greenwich Observatory.*

### TRANSIT

*The only practical way of measuring a sidereal day (one absolute revolution of the Earth) is by observing two successive transits of the same star over the meridian. This is done by a telescope mounted on an East-West axis so that it can only swing in a North-South plane. The observer times the instant at which the star crosses the centre of his sights, by reference to the beats of his pendulum clock. All clock time in the world is regulated on this invariable period, by the transit instruments of observatories, with due compensation for various factors.*

*The transit, meridian circle and clock were the instruments on which exact astronomy was founded, but with changes in technology and in observatory programmes of work, the first two were merged in the transit circle which then superseded them as the standard observatory apparatus.*

# Chapter 3: William Simms – From Small Beginnings

WILLIAM SIMMS (1793-1860) CAME FROM a family which was comfortably established in the middle ranks of the trade. Like others of this class, they moved around from place to place and within the mechanical trades, as opportunity and finances dictated. This mobility, allied to the family preference for the names 'James' and 'William', makes their history difficult to trace. There were members of the Simms family living in the City of London in the last quarter of the 18th century. Some of these were freemen of the Butchers' Company, a number of them still working as butchers, whilst others in the jewellery trade were free of the Goldsmith's Company. The William Simms who entered into partnership with Edward Troughton was the second of that name to make his living in the scientific instruments trade. He was born in Birmingham where his father William Simms (1763-1828) made small metal goods, ornaments and trinkets. In 1794 the family moved to London where the father became a maker of marine compasses. In 1808 William was apprenticed to Thomas Penstone, a working goldsmith, and turned over to his father the following year to complete his apprenticeship. He was made free in the Goldsmiths Company in 1815. Of his brothers, John Simms served his apprenticeship with Richard Sibley, a silversmith, and was made free in 1819; George, James and his son William, set up home and workshop in Greville Street, Clerkenwell, where they advertised themselves as marine compass makers, until 1859. Frederick Walter Simms (1803-65) was bound to Robert Wilmott, cabinet maker, but turned over to his father and made free in 1825; Alfred Septimus Simms was bound to his brother William and made free in 1828. We see here a family all concerned, one way or another, in precision metalworking, and, in the 1820s, established at Bowman's Buildings, off Aldersgate Street in the City of London.

Soon after obtaining his freedom, William sent details of his 'improved protractor' to the Royal Society of Arts, supported by a letter from Thomas Jones (1775-1852), one of Ramsden's former workmen. The Society's Mechanics' Committee were inclined to award him a prize, but before doing so, they prudently consulted Dudley Adams (1762-1830), maker of protractors for the Ordnance. Adams' report was critical of the protractor's usefulness and the Society lost interest in it. Many years later, when an Indian surveyor sent him designs for a similar protractor, William recalled this episode.

We have William's own statement that his first exercise on a dividing engine had been a two-feet circle for a transit. At this time there were about 10 or 12 dividing engines in the London trade, so it cannot be taken for granted that this exercise was done on one of the Troughton machines. His next commission, however, almost certainly was, for it was to repair and redivide the fine astronomical circle which Troughton had constructed for John Pond in 1800 (mentioned in Chapter 2). After 25 years' exposure, for a time to the destructive London air, parts of its brasswork had simply perished. William replaced the metal, redivided the limbs, and shortened the telescope; thus repaired the circle passed

# The Simms Family

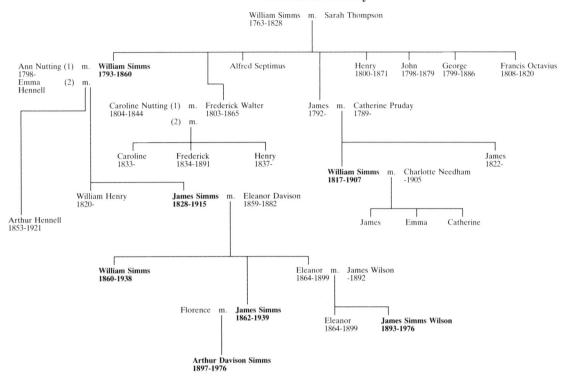

into the hands of a Dr Scott of Bedford Square. A paper that William wrote for Edward Troughton, in which he proposed a method of dividing that was more accurate than by engine yet less tedious than by the roller, demonstrates his keen interest in the various methods of dividing as they were then practised in the workshops of London and Paris, for by this time published descriptions were available for study.

Indeed, during the 1820s the whole tenor of London working-class life was changing, in line with that elsewhere in the country, where the younger craftsmen were part of a general movement for self-improvement. Artisans' classes and institutions were being organised,

though many enjoyed but a fleeting existence. This wish for self-betterment was encouraged by the more enlightened engineering employers, for a workman who could read instructions and understand a working drawing was more valuable than an illiterate. Alfred, Henry and William Simms (and two of the Fayrer family) were members of the London Mechanics Institution, founded in 1824. There they joined a circle of around 1,500 like-minded mechanics, trandesmen and clerks, meeting at first in a disused chapel in Monkswell Street, off London Wall, then in premises off Chancery Lane, both within easy reach of the various Simms' workshops. The Institution offered classes in

*William Simms (1793-1860).*

*William Simms (1817-1905). From MHS Oxford, 37-42.*

*Frederick William Simms (1833-1891).*

mathematics, physics, chemistry, mechanics, optics and astronomy, besides encouraging its members to broaden their general knowledge by the study of geography, history, music and French language. William Simms attended classes from the autumn of 1825 until December 1829.

———

The great Greenwich transit, completed in 1816, was the last major work to come from Troughton's hand. A three-feet circle, intended for St Petersburg but countermanded due to fears of an impending Napoleonic attack on that city, was bought by Troughton's friend William Pearson. It took 10 years to complete Pearson's order, and when Troughton fell ill, Thomas Jones divided its circles, to Troughton's entire satisfaction. Notwithstanding this illness, Troughton was able to travel to France in the autumn of 1824, spending some time at Passy, near Paris, where his friend Sir James South had an observatory, then visiting Paris, before returning to London early in 1825.

When Simms was taken into partnership in 1826, he and his family left the Islington house that they had shared with his father and came to live at 136 Fleet Street. His wife, Ann Nutting, was the sister of John Nutting, William's second apprentice, and of Caroline Nutting, who married his brother Frederick. John Nutting came with them to Fleet Street and for one term he too attended the Mechanics Institution.

There was no shortage of orders in hand when in 1827 a letter came from the Edinburgh Astronomical Institution (probably at the suggestion of its patron, Sir Thomas MakDougall Brisbane) asking Troughton's advice as to the best size and form of mural circle and altazimuth circle for the Calton Hill Observatory. Troughton recommended a six-feet mural circle, to cost 700 guineas, and a three-feet altazimuth circle, to cost 400 guineas. He and Simms considered that both instruments would be ready by the midsummer of 1829, the altazimuth probably before this date. H.M. Treasury approved the estimate, and the order was given to

*Telescopes by Troughton & Simms and Cooke on the terrace of Sir William Keith Murray's Auchtertyre Observatory.*

Adie who was closely involved with the Astronomical Institution in that city, sent his son John Adie (1805-57) to London to familiarise himself with the altazimuth and its arrangement. This opportunity to spend a month in one of the great London workshops must have been turned to good account, and doubtless John learned much more than simply how to adjust a new instrument, before he and it took ship back to Leith. The mural circle languished until 1834 when Simms began to divide its circles. It was finally set up and pronounced satisfactory in September that year.

The reason that the Edinburgh commissions were neglected was that George (later Sir George) Everest (1790-1866) of the Indian Trigonometrical Survey was in London, pressing Troughton & Simms to deal with his considerable needs, and at the same time, Colby and Drummond urgently wanted specialised equipment for the Survey of Ireland. Then, as now, the man who hammers on the shop counter gets priority.

Ramsden's old three-foot theodolite was still in fine fettle and served for the primary triangulations of the Irish Survey. A two-foot theodolite, engine-divided, was commissioned from Troughton & Simms and supplemented it from 1827. In an unfortunate mishap early in the following year, this instrument fell over and suffered damage. It was returned to London, where the damage was found to be so severe that Simms had to redivide it by hand. Whilst this theodolite was under construction, Simms had made several standard bars for the survey, two wrought iron bars each 10 feet long, and others of shorter length, all carefully divided by dots on inset silver discs. At various times, William Yolland and Thomas Drummond enlisted Simms' help to compare these bars with other standards available in London, including that made by Troughton in 1792. Together, Colby, Drummond and Simms designed and built the 'Colby Bars' with their ingenious means of temperature compensation, by which the principal baseline in Ireland was measured. Simms made six sets of Colby Bars for various surveys.

Troughton & Simms in March 1827. A lengthy silence ensued. In June 1830 an emissary from Edinburgh reported that neither instrument was complete; a year had passed, during which time the skeleton of the mural circle had stood untouched, as Simms was fully occupied with instruments for the Survey of India. The altazimuth was ready by August 1830, but Simms, who under the terms of the contract should have accompanied it north and seen to its erection and adjustments, claimed that he was too busy to leave London. Consequently, the renowned Edinburgh instrument maker Alexander

Captain (as he then was) Everest had returned to Britain from India in 1828 and he first went over to Ireland to see what he could usefully learn about current surveying methods. He compiled long reports to his masters, the Honourable East India Company, and asked that Troughton & Simms might repair the old three-feet theodolite then in India, and prepare sets of baseline apparatus, various lamps, theodolites both large and small, levels, and sundry other equipment. There were already numerous surveying instruments, of varying ages and reliability, belonging to the three Presidencies of Bengal, Bombay and Madras, which undertook their own local topographical and revenue surveys. The Great Trigonometrical Survey of India desired instruments of the very best quality, to generate the primary network on which future maps of all India would depend. This was of course a long-running project and Simms' immediate concern in 1829 was to gratify Everest's demands for a new pattern of theodolite to his own design, and to press on with the altazimuth circle under construction. Everest wished both faces of its vertical circle to be divided, and, anticipating objections to the additional expense, he invited Francis Baily, J. F. W. Herschel, James South and no doubt other notables into Simms' shop to examine the piece and to pronounce in support of his proposals. Simms had his say, but at the end of the day was prepared to do what was asked of him, and to charge accordingly – the extra graduation plus reading microscopes would cost the Company an additional £157.

Theodolites, and indeed all surveying apparatus, had a rough tough life in the Indian field. Packed and unpacked repeatedly, carried up and down towers and exposed to extremes of heat and humidity, they inevitably suffered bumps and knocks which could seldom be repaired in India. Damaged instruments were returned to London for attention, which meant that they were out of commission for many months. Everest believed that if small-sized theodolites could be built with a lower centre of gravity, they would be more compact and thus less likely to suffer accident. After touring the scientific instrument shops of the city and finding nothing that met with his approval, he returned to Fleet Street to discuss the matter with Simms. Together they confected the 'East India Company Model' generally known thereafter as the 'Everest' theodolite. It was immediately popular and not being patented, could and was manufactured by anyone who so wished. They also designed the powerful reflector lamps which would be placed on the tops of survey towers, for sighting across country at night. (It was seldom possible to get a clear view across some 50 miles of hot shimmering air during the day.)

Everest then returned to India, no doubt to the relief of all at 136 Fleet Street. Yet the business of building new and highly accurate apparatus continued, as the Survey of Ireland progressed. Other engineers knocked on the door with their ideas. William Gravatt brought along his designs for a small level, and a levelling staff, which Troughton & Simms made in considerable numbers.

––––––––––

Whereas Edward Troughton had not advertised his wares, Troughton & Simms were well-served in this respect by William's brother Frederick Walter Simms. Having served an apprenticeship with his father, Frederick spent some time on the Irish Survey and then became Assistant at Greenwich Observatory. He found Airy's new regime uncongenial, and moved into the more lucrative profession of railway engineer. He wrote several books on surveying and the use of instruments, aimed at the fast-expanding body of civil engineers. His first book, published in 1834, referred to several Troughton & Simms products, notably the Everest theodolite, Troughton's level and levelling staff, Troughton's mountain barometer, reflecting circle, portable transit and dip sector, all instruments necessary for the field engineer. At the end of the book was a price-list of the books and instruments sold at 136 Fleet Street. In 1845 Frederick was appointed consulting engineer to the Government of India, whence he departed for five years, so that some later editions of his books, which were also published in America and translated for European consumption, were backed with other makers' catalogues.

Edward Troughton, by now in his seventies, troubled by rheumatism and lumbago and by all accounts rather deaf, was cared for by Mrs Simms at 136 Fleet Street, but he was certainly not simply a sleeping partner. Everest found him a reasonable and compliant man, and was happy to do business with him. Indeed, after discussing with Everest the construction of geodetic pendulums, used by surveyors to calculate the local force of gravity, Troughton went away and began work on one of his own design.

On the other hand, the previously close friendship with Sir James South was brought, through the obstinacy of both men, to a stormy and bitter end. South, a wealthy and competent amateur astronomer, had over the years acquired a number of instruments from Troughton, for whom he had the highest regard. Troughton had maintained the instruments in South's various observatories, the most recent being on Campden Hill, in Kensington. South's independent status allowed him to campaign against the inaction and policies of the Royal Society, the Royal Astronomical Society, and other organisations and persons whose actions annoyed him. These campaigns brought him both friends and enemies and when he fell into dispute with Edward Troughton, there were plenty of eminent men prepared to take sides. The dispute came about in this way. South already possessed a superb equatorial telescope mounted by James Huddart and the Troughtons, with a lens of $3\frac{3}{4}$ inches aperture, but he yearned for something better, equivalent to the best telescopes now being made in Germany. At last, in 1829, he was able to buy a lens made by Cauchoix in Paris, a veritable masterpiece, having $11\frac{3}{4}$ inches clear aperture. He took this lens to Edward Troughton, asking him to make a scaled-up version of the old equatorial, but Troughton declared this to be impractical and he insisted on an entirely different mounting. The process of constructing this telescope was afterwards set down by William Simms, and his essay shows what the normal procedure was for a large instrument of this class, and the parts played by the purchaser, maker, and sub-contractors. Briefly, a cabinet maker named Norton constructed a quarter-scale wooden model which was adjusted until South and Troughton were satisfied with the design. South insisted that this model be set up in Troughton's bedroom, lest it should be seen by his astronomical rivals. Norton then made full-size gauges of the axis, which were sent to the timber yard as a guide to cutting the timber. South tried to obtain some teak from a government store, but was unsuccessful and had to accept mahogany. Donkin was to make the brass tube and other large metal parts, but instead of making the tube after the axis had been prepared, South urged him to complete it so that he could use it on a temporary support, and it had been finished in December 1829. Meanwhile, Norton was building the axis, Fayrer was making the drive clock, and Troughton and Simms and their lesser sub-contractors were busy with their respective portions. Throughout 1830 and most of 1831 South was in and out of all the workshops almost daily, and in fact hindering the work by continually demanding modifications to the finders, micrometers, and so forth. In particular, he persuaded Edward Troughton against the latter's better judgement to increase the size of the declination circle from 10 or 12 inches to two feet. In the summer of 1831 the axis was taken to Donkin's factory to have the metal pivots turned and at this stage it was discovered that its joints had shrunk and become loose. At Donkin's suggestion it was strengthened with cast iron ties. In September it was taken to Campden Hill and South's builder came to organise its lifting, which was to be supervised by a Captain Robertson RN. With the upper pivot only inches from its place, the tackle gave way and the instrument fell several feet, the upper end of the pivot shattering the framework of the dome, and the lower end crashing onto a stone block. The impact further weakened the axis. Other tackle was brought, and the telescope then lifted into its correct place.

*Sir James South's telescope dismantled for sale at his Campden Hill observatory, 1839.*

Alas, when it was tried out, the telescope had so unsteady a motion that the stars appeared to float across the field of view. South wrote a formal letter accusing Troughton of constructing 'a useless pile' and calling on him to make it into an instrument worthy of them both.

While Troughton considered how to remedy this defect, South and his carpenter were also tinkering with the telescope. Donkin thought that the lower bearing was the cause of the trouble, given the great weight of the telescope, and several modifications were tried, but with little improvement. Relationships deteriorated further; South imposed endless petty restrictions on Troughton and his workmen. There was general embarrassment, particularly for Troughton's friends Richard Sheepshanks and George Airy, who now attempted a rescue operation to save him from further professional and financial disaster. Sheepshanks' legal training was invaluable when the matter was delivered into the hands of solicitors. It was agreed that Troughton & Simms were to have a short period to set matters right, whereupon the result would be assessed by a group of professional astronomers. Voices were still being raised in argument when Edward Troughton died in June 1835. Simms and the Troughton faction battled on to achieve a sort of victory in 1836.

———

Edward Troughton had never married. His estate was valued at £12,000. He bequeathed some £700 to each of his various nephews and nieces and their families. He also left £336 (less tax) to the St Bride's Parish School, and a like sum to the London Vaccine Institute. Sothebys auctioned off his extensive library, his few 'antiquities' and pictures, and the instruments which had been his private possessions, along with bits and pieces that had probably been on his bench when he died. Simms bought a few of the technical books, and most of the instruments, along with Edward's fishing rods. The business of Troughton & Simms did not figure in the Will, having presumably been transferred to William Simms by a previous legal settlement, and Simms received only a token bequest, although a codicil added £100 for his wife, in recognition of her care for the old man in his last years. When the Will was proved, James Fayrer, who had married Troughton's niece in 1798, put in a claim for work done between 1803 and 1826, to the value of £573-0-6d. He had left Troughton to decide on the payment due for each of the instruments made to Troughton's instructions, content to let these sums accumulate, in effect using Troughton as his savings bank. All work done by Fayrer after Troughton took Simms into partnership in March 1826 had been paid promptly. The subject of these payments had been raised during Troughton's lifetime, but no settlement had been made. Fortunately for Fayrer, his circumstances were well-known, and he received all that was due to him.

After Troughton had been buried, according to his wishes, in the new Kensal Green Cemetery, business continued as before for William Simms. Prudently, he continued to trade as Troughton & Simms, the name still having value, especially for overseas buyers. Simms' immediate task was to forge a relationship in his own right with George Biddell Airy (1801-1892), former Director of the Cambridge Observatory, elevated to the post of Astronomer Royal in 1835.

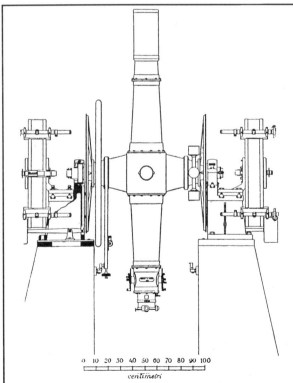

*TRANSIT CIRCLE*

*An instrument for timing a star's meridian passage, at the same time measuring its angular distance from the zenith. The Transit Circle was set with its axis aligned East-West, and a clock or chronograph nearby. Observations of a star's transit were at first timed by listening to the beat of the clock. In later years, the observer pressed an electric key at the instant of transit and the event was recorded alongside a time-trace on the chronograph.*

*Edward Troughton constructed the first transit circle for Stephen Groombridge in 1806, but the design was not then adopted in Britain, though it became popular on the continent. The first British circle was made to Airy's design for Greenwich Observatory and was mounted in 1850. A complex system of levers and counterpoises transferred most of the instrument's weight from the pivots to the piers. There are one or two divided circles, graduated on inset bands of silver or other fine metal, and read by four or more micrometer microscopes, their readings then being averaged to eliminate errors.*

0 10 20 30 40 50 60 70 80 90 100
*centimetri*

# Chapter 4: Standards of Precision – The Simms Family at Fleet Street

WILLIAM SIMMS WAS NOW IN SOLE command of a thriving firm, and personally attending to the needs of his major institutional customers. Orders came in from the Board of Ordnance and East India Company, from new observatories in America and Europe, and from civil engineers. When Professor Airy of Cambridge was appointed Astronomer Royal he swept into Greenwich bringing new methods of management, new ideas about the function of the Royal Observatory, and new plans for instruments. Astronomer, engineer, mathematician and administrator, Airy's tenure at Greenwich lasted from 1835 to 1881, and embroiled him in most of the influential scientific activities of the time. One way or another, work for Airy came to dominate both the time and resources of the Simms family, within the Greenwich Observatory itself and during the reconstruction of the national standards of length after a fire at the Houses of Parliament had destroyed the originals. Somehow William had to find time for the court case against Sir James South, mentioned earlier, and to greet the various high-powered foreign visitors who regarded the Troughton & Simms shop as an essential stop on the London scientific circuit.

The precision engineering for this increased volume of trade was carried out in the works of Maudslay & Field and Donkin, both situated on the south bank of the Thames, and by Ransomes & May in distant Ipswich, from which castings arrived by ship. In Fleet Street, William Simms' sons William Henry (b1820) and James (1828-1919) were bound apprentice to him in 1834 and 1843 respectively, while his nephew William (1817-1907)

joined him in 1836. William Henry was admitted to Pembroke College, Cambridge, in 1838 but illness interrupted his studies. He went to Ireland to recuperate, returning to Cambridge in 1840 but in 1841 he was expelled 'for contumacy'. After this unfortunate episode he went to Ceylon as a surveyor. William's brother-in-law John Nutting kept the books until his early death around 1837. Henry Simms (b1800) succeeded to this post. In 1846 he took as apprentice Joseph Beck, the fee of 200 guineas for this binding reflecting his high status as a practitioner.

William Simms continued to employ Troughton's method of 'dividing by eye' on his most important circles, and in 1834 he addressed the Institution of Civil Engineers (he had been a Member since 1828) on the Edinburgh mural circle, and dividing generally. The question of mechanical copy-dividing seems to have occupied much of his time; Ferdinand Hassler had ordered a six-feet dividing engine in 1833, which with delays and modifications took nearly 10 years to complete. On arrival in America, it was found to have been very carelessly made and an American instrument maker named Joseph Saxton had to rebuild it for Hassler. At the same time Simms was fitting a self-acting mechanism to Troughton's dividing engine. These trials paid off when he came to build his own dividing engine, which was completed in 1843 and received much acclaim. The engine was driven, like clockwork, by a falling weight which moved down the exterior wall in Peterborough Court. William Simms was not secretive about his ideas and inventions, and described them in

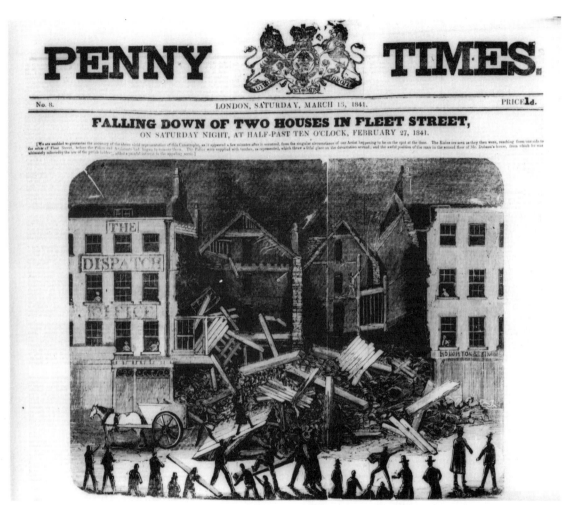

# PENNY TIMES.

No. 8.                    LONDON, SATURDAY, MARCH 13, 1841.                    PRICE **1d.**

## FALLING DOWN OF TWO HOUSES IN FLEET STREET,

### ON SATURDAY NIGHT, AT HALF-PAST TEN O'CLOCK, FEBRUARY 27, 1841.

[We are enabled to guarantee the accuracy of the above vivid representation of this Catastrophe, as it appeared a few minutes after it occurred, from the singular circumstance of our Artist happening to be on the spot at the time. The Ruins are seen as they then were, reaching from one side to the other of Fleet Street, before the Police and Assistants had begun to remove them. The Police were supplied with torches, as represented, which threw a fitful glare on the devastation around; and the awful position of the man in the second floor of Mr. Dobson's house, from which he was ultimately relieved by the use of the parish ladders, added a painful interest to the appalling scene.]

*Collapse of 137 and 138 Fleet Street in February 1841.*

papers and books, but he did not file any patents relating to them.

Other duties devolved on the Simms family, as Fleet Street residents. William Simms served as Constable of St Bride's parish in 1836 and as a Trustee from 1836 to 1839. James Simms held vestry office in 1843. There were excitements too – in January 1841 a fire burnt out the rear of No. 138 Fleet Street. The insurance company repaired the premises, but in the evening of Saturday 27 February the front parts of 138 and 137 collapsed into the street, fortunately without loss of life. Simms' neighbour in Peterborough Court helped him to clear

*James Simms (1828-1915).*

the land, which extended back into Peterborough Court. This reconstruction was undertaken during 1842-43, and by 1844 Simms was settled in his new premises of 138 Fleet Street (not forgetting a new rooftop observatory), with another two houses in the Court behind.

After the death of William's wife he married Emma Hennell. (Her family was in business with that of his first wife as Hennell & Nutting, jewellers.) Their daughter was born in Fleet Street in 1849 but by the time of the 1851 census he had moved his growing family to a large house at Carshalton, in Surrey. Here he built another observatory, and indulged his interest in astronomy. He had been a Fellow of the Royal Astronomical Society since 1831, serving from time to time on its Council, and joining the Astronomical Dining Club, so that he was a familiar figure in the astronomical world. Sir James South is unlikely to have been amongst his friends. The dispute was settled in 1836, in favour of Troughton & Simms. The irate South smashed the telescope into useless parts which he advertised as scrap metal and wood in a display of petulance that amused both the locals and the trade, and he continued his battle of wills against the unfortunate Sheepshanks who had taken Troughton's part in the whole sorry affair.

––––––––

Orders flowed from overseas. Hassler commissioned another large theodolite which was ready by 1836. It was put on display in the shop where, Hassler's agent reported, it was so much admired that Simms was reluctant to pack it up for shipment. In 1838 Hassler returned the worn-out Troughton theodolite of 1815 for repair. When Charles Wilkes of the United States Navy came to London in 1836 to outfit the planned US Exploring Expedition, he found all the top London craftsmen so busy that until some kind-hearted private individuals withdrew their orders, he could not be served. At the time, Simms was constructing the optical and graduated parts for Cambridge University's mighty 'Northumberland' telescope with its Cauchoix lens, and he took Wilkes with him to Cambridge to meet some of

the shop, in case there was further damage, but in the event only a portion of the coping fell down. The police arrived, then the builders came and shored up his wall. Business, as Simms dryly explained to Airy, was disrupted for some days. But good came of the accident. No. 138 Fleet Street was the property of St Bride's parish. The previous owner was persuaded to surrender his lease and Simms negotiated with the vestry and the Hand-in-Hand Insurance Company to lease 138 Fleet Street for 80 years at a rent of £150 per annum free of Land Tax, from Christmas 1841. Simms was to receive the insurance payment of £1,200 and would spend a further £1,500, erecting a house and other buildings on its resident scientists. Writing home to his wife after they had shared lodgings there, Wilkes reported – with some surprise – that Simms was quite an amusing companion. Troughton & Simms supplied his expedition with a telescope and various surveying instruments. The same year Professor Elias Loomis came to buy a transit and an equatorial for his college in Ohio. In 1851 Don Saturnino Montojo, Director of the Spanish Naval Observatory at Cadiz, left an order for philosophical teaching apparatus. In 1854 King Pedro V of Portugal and his Surveyor-General Felipe Folque came to Britain, and amongst a round of royal entertainments found time to visit Greenwich Observatory and call on London's best instrument makers. On 15 June, Folque left his King enjoying a day at the races with Queen Victoria and betook himself to Troughton & Simms, where he admired an excellent standard barometer, priced at 20 guineas.

In 1838 complaints about 'Gilbert's rattletraps' led the East India Company to reconsider the procedure for designing and supplying instruments. Gilbert's name was struck off the 'approved' list and, on Everest's recommendation, Troughton & Simms were appointed to provide the revenue and local surveyors with small theodolites, levels, protractors, and sundry other philosophical and drawing instruments. J. A. Hodgson, Astronomer at Madras and a professed admirer of Simms' skill, came to England on leave and collaborated with him on the design of a compact transit theodolite with five-inch circles, for which Simms received a substantial order.

By 1845 all the large theodolites sent to India during Troughton's lifetime, with the exception of the 36-inch, were worn out. Simms' new dividing engine was now at work and two 24-inch theodolites were ordered. On their arrival in 1847, Andrew Waugh, Surveyor-General from 1843 to 1861, declared them equal to the old hand-divided 36-inch one, though he subsequently added extra microscopes, fitted German levels, and in one case managed to reverse the cone of the axis, in order to tilt the telescope to a higher angle. This dissatisfaction with Simms' levels was to be echoed by Airy, who also declared German levels to be far superior to any made in England.

In Britain, the Board of Ordnance ordered drawing and surveying instruments for the Royal Military Academy, Woolwich, as well as for the Ordnance Survey, now in sight of completing the first national triangulation. Simms' journal shows that some of these instruments were made to designs submitted by staff at the Academy. Young William was given the job of redividing the old Ramsden 18-inch theodolite, which was set up on the top of St Paul's Cathedral as the triangulation was carried across London.

The opening of the Stockton and Darlington Railway in 1825, and the Liverpool and Manchester Railway in 1830, heralded the frenetic railway manias of the 1840s. By 1852, when the dust of battle had largely subsided, 7,500 route miles of track had actually been built, though many times that number had been surveyed after a fashion. To secure the necessary Act of Parliament, companies had to submit plans of their proposed route. Successful companies then made detailed surveys in order to construct the bridges, cuttings, embankments, and diversion of waterways, ancillary to the graded track. The manpower shortage led to some dreadful abuses of the surveyors' art. Ordnance Survey maps were cribbed, and proper training was replaced by hasty learning from the 20-odd books on railway surveying published between 1840 and 1850 (Frederick Walter Simms' among them). Tales abound of theodolites and levels being smashed by irate landowners and bands of men hired by competing companies. It was all good for business, for the repair and trade-in of second-hand instruments had always gone along with the supply of new ones. A Brunel or a Rennie could afford the latest designs and highest quality from Troughton & Simms; a humble beginner made do with a reconditioned piece for his first job.

———

The manufacture of standards of length absorbed a share of both time and space at Fleet Street. By their nature, standards were expected to endure, if not for ever, at least for many years. The length was defined at a standard temperature, usually 62°F, for everyone knew that metal expanded with heat. Consequently the problem facing Simms was to find a durable material which, under changing temperatures, altered its length at a known rate. Earlier standards were of brass, but 'brass' could refer to any one of several mixtures, each with a different rate of expansion and all liable to corrode. Iron was no better in this respect. Platinum did not corrode, but its rates of expansion were uncertain. Glass was tried but found wanting. Given a suitable alloy, it was the instrument-maker's task to prepare and mark out a bar of the desired length, and then to carry out a series of measurements with the bar heated to different temperatures, to discover how its length altered.

Simms already had experience of making and testing a standard, for he had made five tubular scales between 1833 and 1835. No. 1, for the Royal Astronomical Society, had been taken to the Houses of Parliament, to compare it with Donkin's own and the old standard yard of 1760. The comparisons were made in a Committee Room with a northern aspect, where the temperature would be stable. Tubular scale No. 2 was made for Schumacher, for Denmark, No. 3 for Struve, for Russia, No. 4, six feet long, for the 'Euphrates Expedition' of 1835 which went in search of an overland route to India, and No. 5 for the astronomer Francis Baily (1774-1844).

In 1839 comparisons were made in the cellar of Simms' premises between the 10-foot Ordnance bar and those destined for the Cape of Good Hope Observatory. In these tests Simms was assisted by members of the Royal Astronomical Society, the Board of Ordnance, Bryan Donkin's son and his own nephew. The comparisons, which were repeated hour after hour, day after day, with the bars' temperatures, the atmospheric pressure and temperature all noted, must have been wearisome in the extreme, but were absolutely essential to provide a reliable measure by which entire countries would be mapped. By contrast, to check the surveying chains which he supplied in quantity to private and government order, Simms simply drove two brass plugs into the pavement outside his workshop, and marked off the exact distance of one chain, or 66 feet, between their centres.

In 1834 fire had destroyed the Houses of Parliament, where the British primary standards were stored. In due course a Commission was appointed to consider how these standards should be recreated. After much consultation, the Commissioners abandoned their earlier belief that the standard yard could be reconstituted from the 'natural' length of a pendulum beating seconds, recommending instead that the new yard should be prepared from those in private and institutional hands. It was to be made by William Simms, under the instructions of a working party which included Airy and Baily.

Baily died in 1844, before matters had progressed far. Sheepshanks replaced him on the working party. In 1845 Maudslay & Field cast a number of gunmetal bars, varying slightly in composition, and delivered them to Fleet Street where Simms and Donkin tested their strength and rigidity by loading them to destruction. Forty bars of the best metal were then prepared as line standards. There followed the time-consuming part of the trials, when each bar in turn was put on a roller frame and lowered into a tank of water, heated by spirit lamps, so that its expansion could be measured. The scene of operations was a deep cellar under the Royal Astronomical Society's rooms in Somerset House. In these dank chilly surroundings, lit by Argand lamps, the Simmses, Bryan Donkin, Warren de la Rue, and two assistants from the Greenwich Observatory, took turns at the microscopes. Sheepshanks awarded the palm to young William Simms, saying that one of his observations was worth two by anyone else, and he proposed the young man for election to the Royal Astronomical Society in 1851. Sheepshanks himself died in 1855, shortly before the end was reached. When Airy came to examine the results, he found that nearly 200,000 readings had been made in the previous 10 years.

The best of the bars – that whose expansion most closely matched that of the 'lost' standard – was denominated the 'Imperial Standard'. Others were sent to major cities in the United Kingdom and Colonies, and to foreign governments for exchange with their own standards.

---

Whilst all this was going on, a succession of large astronomical instruments was being shipped off to observatories at home and overseas. There is room here to mention only a few. A mural circle replicating that at Greenwich, costing 700 guineas, was ordered in 1827 for the Brussels Observatory. Delayed by the Belgian revolution, Simms reported difficulties in its division in 1835; it was delivered later that year and followed by an equatorial costing 450 guineas. In the autumn of 1832 William Simms spent six weeks at Cambridge University Observatory, hand-dividing an eight-feet mural circle on its own axis in order to ensure that the divisions were truly centred. This circle cost the University 1,000 guineas. A mural circle went to Trivandrum, Madras in 1836 and another to Lucknow in 1839 (to be lost in the mutiny of 1857). There were the optical parts and circles for the 'Northumberland' equatorial; delayed by Simms' illness, it was put into operation at Cambridge Observatory late in 1838. In 1843 he rebuilt the frame of a transit that John Bird had made for the Radcliffe Observatory, Oxford, in 1771, replacing the worn parts with a new gunmetal casting. An equatorial (with castings by Maudslay) went to Liverpool in 1848. To America he sent a mural circle to West Point in 1839; a transit in 1848, and later a mural circle to Harvard; an equatorial in 1843, and later a transit circle, to Tuscaloosa; a transit circle to Georgetown, Washington in 1845. The five-feet circles for Washington and West Point were both cast in one piece by Maudslay. He supplied the optical parts and circles for the Cape Transit, built by Ransomes & May, and a transit and equatorial for Melbourne, Australia, in 1854. In addition, many high quality transits, altazimuths and telescopes were made for amateur astronomers in Britain.

William Simms divided some of these circles himself, and later handed over to young William, who also took charge of the Simms dividing engine. Thus freed from the workshop, William senior went to Paris in 1843 to examine Guinand's furnace for making optical glass. When Harvard Observatory bought two object glasses from Merz of Munich, William went to Germany in 1846 with instructions to select the best for mounting in a telescope. There was endless trouble with the Harvard order. The astronomers complained of Simms' inexplicable delays and failure to answer their letters. In November 1847 they were dismayed by his report that half-way through the division, he had found the casting of the transit circle to be defective, and was obliged to start again. Airy and Sheepshanks were called in to examine the instrument and pronounced it excellent, but the Harvard Treasurer despaired at the erratic costing – 'first £400 then £600 now £500' and when the transit was set up and carefully examined, its graduations were found to be uneven.

Troughton & Simms retained their reputation despite such unfortunate delays and defects and it should be remembered that the business was still operating as it had been in previous times, dependent on precision engineering firms for its castings and turnings, and on local subcontractors for subsidiary parts. There were times when Airy fulminated against Simms' inability to adhere to his estimates, but in all likelihood the larger part of his production costs, both time and materials, was beyond his control.

Some orders were declined: around 1850 the East India Company's Mathematical Instrument Maker's establishment at Calcutta was being re-equipped. The indent included 'a dividing machine with the latest improvements'. Answer came that 'there was but one in England and that in the possession of Messrs Troughton & Simms who state that it took years of thought and study to complete it, that its cost must not be estimated

*Airy's Altazimuth at Greenwich Observatory, the optical parts and the divided circle made by Troughton & Simms, 1847.*

Simms inherited from Troughton the responsibility for cleaning, repairs and adjustments to the Greenwich apparatus. Airy now commissioned a set of magnetic instruments for the Magnetic and Meteorological Observatory, opened in 1838. The first astronomical order came in 1843, for an altazimuth to Airy's design. It was to have a massive stand, cast in as few sections as possible by Ransomes & May of Ipswich, a firm with whom Airy had family ties. Ransomes' move to a new factory delayed the start of the work, but eventually it proceeded, with Simms responsible for the three-foot graduated circles, the telescope, microscope, levels etc, and the Y-shaped supports for the horizontal axis. With the iron parts being cast and turned at Ipswich, the optical and dividing work being done at Fleet Street, and the structure to receive the altazimuth being built at Greenwich, it is no wonder that logistic problems arose. Men, materials, and letters galore went backwards and forwards. Airy came back from France in 1845 and went immediately to Simms' shop to see the instrument, which he liked.. But when it arrived at Greenwich and Airy compared it to his drawings, he found serious errors which entailed its return to Ipswich for correction.

The same team embarked on a similar exercise in 1848, this time for a transit circle, designed round an eight-inch object glass, for which Simms was paid £275. The six-foot long cast-iron axis rested in chilled iron pivots – a technical innovation of which Ransomes were proud. May exhibited a model and described the process of chilling to the British Association meeting at Ipswich in 1851. There was a six-foot vertical circle of iron, into which Simms put a silver band, engine-divided – the first major instrument not to be divided by hand. This excellent instrument defined the Greenwich Meridian from 1851 till 1927.

In 1851 Simms constructed a zenith tube round an object glass that Dollond had made in 1793 for an earlier transit. In 1859 he contributed two circles divided on silver and the optical parts for the 'Great Equatorial' which was designed by Airy, with mountings by Ransomes & Sims (no relation to Simms), an object

under thousands of pounds, and that they altogether declined the task of making another'.

The Great Exhibition of 1851 came at a time when Simms was more than fully occupied and he was only persuaded to enter at the last minute, when someone realised that England's foremost astronomical instrument maker was not among the list of exhibitors. He sent along the old Westbury circle of 1800, recently purchased in a sale at a bargain price, a fine 15-inch altazimuth, engine-divided, some lesser transits and an altazimuth, two telescopes, some small surveying instruments, three imperial standards, and an elliptograph made to Airy's design some 10 years earlier, which had failed to sell.

glass by Merz, and a clock by Dent. Airy came to regard the Simms family as his personal mechanics for any small task, from repairing his spectacles to making up some gadget from his scribbled sketch. In return, from 1842, Simms was invited to attend the Board of Visitors' annual inspection of the Observatory and to dine with them afterwards.

In 1852 Simms published *The achromatic telescope and its various mountings, especially the equatorial, to which are added some hints on private observatories*, a book which offered his customers instruction and advice on getting the best results from their equipment. The same year, 20 leading astronomers and engineers proposed him for election to the Royal Society, testifying that he was 'the author of several papers . . . the inventor of a self-acting machine for dividing circles . . . distinguished for his acquaintance with the science of practical optics and astronomical mechanics . . . eminent as an astronomical observer and as an artist in the construction of philosophical apparatus, telescopes, instruments etc . . .' It was a fitting tribute and accolade to the long and productive life of a man known for his kind, modest and gentle nature.

---

Y Pattern.

Small Transit Pattern.

'Everest' Pattern.

## THEODOLITE

*A surveying instrument to measure vertical angles (altitude) and horizontal angles (azimuth).*

*Altazimuth theodolites of recognisably modern form were made from the early 18th century, and they were soon adapted for hydrographic, topographic and mine surveying. The size of the instrument, which can be as small as three inches or as large as three feet, is taken from the diameter of the azimuth circle. The telescope of a transit theodolite is set high enough to allow it to point directly up or down, which can be useful in mine surveying or astronomy, but makes it top-heavy. The Everest theodolite, with its vertical circle cut down to two arcs, is a compact and stable instrument with a low centre of gravity. Theodolites have improved in accuracy over the years. Originally, the circles were read with the aid of verniers – then with microscopes, and, when the accuracy of the divisions justified it, with micrometer microscopes. The Tavistock and other 20th-century theodolites had their circles divided on glass, with the reading passed through an internal arrangement of lenses and prisms to the eyepiece.*

# Chapter 5: Surveying the World and the Heavens

OLD WILLIAM SIMMS DIED AT Carshalton in the summer of 1860. His estate, which included the assets and goodwill of the firm, was valued at just under £80,000. Far-reaching changes had taken place during his lifetime. London itself had doubled in size. In some respects, the known world had expanded, as new lands were discovered and mapped (often with Troughton & Simms instruments); in other respects it had diminished, with faster communications brought about by a global network of steamship routes and telegraph cables. In the autumn of 1860 William (1817-1907), and his cousin James (1828-1915) entered into a deed of partnership which lasted until William's retirement in 1871, and carried the business into the industrial age.

Little has been said about the manufacture of lenses in earlier chapters. The Troughtons had not made their own (it was said that Edward was colour-blind and therefore not able to judge the clarity of lenses for himself). When the duty on glass was abolished in 1845, British glassworks were encouraged to produce better optical glass. The Simmses began to take an interest in optical technology and to grind their own lenses.

Despite official encouragement to the British manufacturers, it remained for a Swiss amateur telescope maker, Pierre Guinand, to develop a reliable method of preparing clear optical glass. He found that continuous stirring during melting eliminated all bubbles and strain lines. It was a demonstration of this process which William Simms had gone to Paris to see in October 1843. Guinand sold his process to a famous Munich optical glass works, later controlled by Merz, which Simms had also visited in 1846. After Guinand's death, one of his sons went to work for Bontemps in Paris, and in 1848 Bontemps united with Chance Brothers in England.

Glass for optical purposes was not blown or rolled, but allowed to cool slowly in its pot, then removed and broken up. Flawed pieces were discarded, and the remaining blocks cut into discs. These were sent to the optician who ground them to the shape of a lens with perfectly spherical surfaces. The convex face was ground in a saucer-shaped iron plate covered with pitch, hatched by cross-grooves to take away the waste material. The pitch was warmed and covered with rouge – a fine abrasive. The lens was then rubbed and turned by hand or machine to achieve the desired curve.

The first evidence we have of a serious interest in the science of optics comes from the correspondence between Airy and William Simms – probably the younger, though one cannot be certain. Young William had been tutored by Mr Hayward, one-time scholar of Christ's Hospital in the Mathematical School and a Naval Instructor, and had later attended the London Mechanic's Institute, so he was able to undertake the calculations needed to prepare lenses for telescopes, spectroscopes and the other types of optical instruments sold by the firm. James Simms had been apprenticed to his father whilst continuing to attend school, and he too was familiar with optical techniques.

In 1861 Lt-Colonel Alexander Strange (1818-76), formerly employed on the Survey of India where he had

considered himself to be something of an instrument engineer, retired to England and was appointed Surveyor of Instruments to the India Office. He superintended the building of an observatory in Lambeth, where for the first time all instruments were to be tested before shipment, and he also set about designing a great theodolite for the Survey of India, based on ideas conceived in India. This theodolite was not only novel in its design, but would have components made of aluminium-bronze, a new alloy that Strange had seen at the 1862 Exhibition in London. Metallurgical experiments carried out at the Woolwich Gun Factory and at Troughton & Simms' led Strange to the entirely mistaken conclusion that aluminium bronze would be the ideal material as it was more rigid than gunmetal but was generally strong and easily worked. Simms was likewise mistaken when he reported to Strange that it would not be necessary to inlay another metal to take the graduations since he had been able to cut the finest divisions on his sample. He also found that it had 'amazing resistance to corrosion'.

Three years later, Strange had to admit that the alloy would not take graduations, that it did tarnish, and that when cast it had an unsound surface. Troughton & Simms spent 10 years over the creation of their three-foot theodolite, delays being attributed to their need to buy and install a new machine tool to handle the job, by their move to new premises at Charlton, and because

each component needed lengthy testing. In the end, the theodolite had few bronze components, being principally cast from the usual gunmetal. Whether for this reason, or due to Strange's design, the great theodolite was condemned as too heavy for Indian surveys and it was despatched to South Africa.

---

By the 1860s, the Fleet Street premises were wholly inadequate for modern machinery and in 1864 the partners bought two acres of land on the Woolwich Road, conveniently located between the Greenwich

*Latitude observations in India, c1890, with a zenith telescope by Troughton & Simms, from* Great Trigonometrical Survey, **18**, *(1906); 16.*

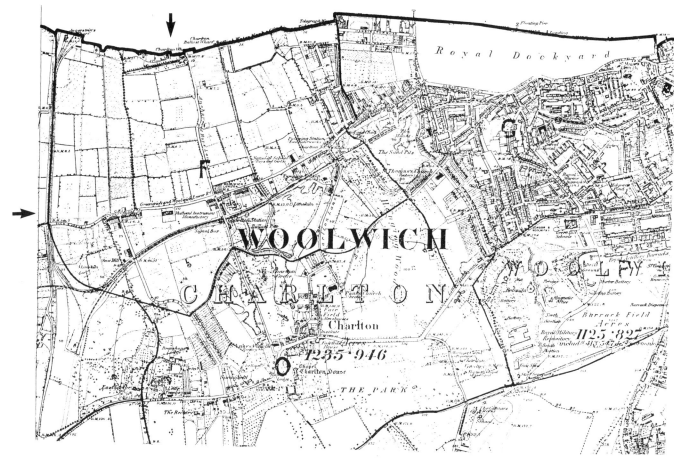

*Charlton c1877, with Troughton & Simms' Works.*

Observatory and the Royal Military Academy in Woolwich Dockyard, two of their major customers. The factory was operating by 1866. In 1871 it was employing 61 men and 18 boys, a number which increased by 1881 to 78 men and 20 boys. In 1866 the Peterborough Court workshops were vacated, but 138 Fleet Street was retained as the Troughton & Simms shop until the lease expired in 1921.

Besides the standard instruments listed in Troughton & Simms' catalogue of 1864, large transit circles were built to order, for the second-generation of national observatories that were springing up in the colonies. These orders were often channelled through Airy, who was asked to recommend a maker and oversee construction. Mural circles were a thing of the past. When the Cambridge mural circle needed attention in 1860, James

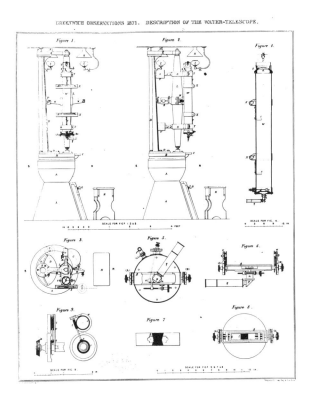

*Diagram of the 'water telescope' made by Troughton & Simms for Greenwich Observatory, 1870, from Airy,* Greenwich Observations, *1871.*

Simms wrote to Professor Challis, 'It is so long since we constructed a mural circle that I should be afraid to entrust the repairs of one to any man at present in our employ without examining the instrument myself.' Cambridge Observatory benefitted under the Sheepshanks Bequest, which paid for an excellent transit circle made by James Simms – or we may perhaps suppose, constructed under his supervision – and mounted in 1867.

Universities and official observatories in North America continued to buy from Troughton & Simms, despite some unsatisfactory experiences. Joseph Winlock, Director of Harvard Observatory from 1866, ordered a spectroscope and a transit from Troughton & Simms. In January 1869, after the promised delivery date had come and gone, Simms wrote that it was completed, but five months later it was still only 'nearly finished' and it did not reach Harvard until the summer of 1870.

America did not have the monopoly of poor service: in Scotland, Charles Piazzi Smyth (1819-1900), Astronomer Royal for Scotland, and David Gill (1843-1914), in charge of Lord Lindsey's private observatory at Dunecht, both endured repeated delays and prevarications over the delivery of their orders. Nor was Piazzi Smyth much pleased when, due to visit London in 1875, he wrote to James Simms asking for an appointment, only to be told that Simms was occupied and 'could not attend to anything but his legitimate business'. 'An answer in rather repelling character' was Piazzi Smyth's verdict. In North America and in Europe the principal competitor was the long-established German firm of Reichenbach. Further south, Troughton & Simms had supplied a zenith telescope and an altazimuth to the Mexican observatory of Chapultepec. For reasons which the embarrassed Mexican government never did elucidate, the altazimuth was delayed and failed to appear in time for the grand formal opening of the observatory in 1878. Despite this ill-omen, they ordered a transit circle for the new observatory at Tacubaya, just outside Mexico City, and this was under construction at Charlton in 1882. At Greenwich, Airy experimented with new types of apparatus and modifications of existing ones, revealing his thoughts in a lively correspondence with the Simms partners. James Simms often took himself abroad, preaching his version of the Christian faith beyond the walls of the chapel that he had built beside the Charlton Works. It is difficult to know what proportion of these absences might have been 'official' business and how much was, as William's daughter claimed, devoted to his self-imposed missionary service in Italy, Spain and Madeira. It was, in her opinion, grossly unfair, since James, as the son of the

43

former proprietor, took two-thirds of the profits, leaving the hard-working and conscientious William with one-third.

———

*Standards of length by Troughton & Simms, set in the wall of the Guildhall in 1878 for the Corporation of London.*

Standards of length contributed to the business, with many overseas governments exchanging standards with Britain. The British Government sanctioned the use of the metric system in 1864 and the Simmses made several metric bars. The Commissioners for the Restoration of the Standards' recommendation that bars be set up in public places for the benefit of tradesmen and merchants wishing to check their own measures was followed in London by the emplacement in 1876 of a set of bars, and studs marking yards, chains and perches, on the north side of Trafalgar Square. In 1878 the Corporation of London followed suit, immuring a set of standards inside Guildhall. Drawing instruments and specialised apparatus was supplied to the Royal Military Academy, conveniently located nearby at Woolwich. There was a buoyant trade in nautical instruments – sextants, station pointers and charting instruments – for the Royal Navy and for merchant seamen. In India, civil engineers were laying roads and railways, building bridges and harbours, and setting up their own training schools and workshops, all of which called for prodigious quantities of apparatus and instruments. The Indian government and the Survey

of India still called for equipment of all sorts. Troughton & Simms enjoyed a virtual monopoly of supply to the Indian government, and it was this monopoly that Lt-Colonel Strange proposed to break, for he felt that it put the firm in too strong a position. Nevertheless, despite his enquiries, Strange was unable to find anyone else who could meet the same standards, until, as we shall see, he came upon Thomas Cooke's display stand at the 1862 Exhibition.

William retired in 1871, to end his days at Shanklin, on the Isle of Wight. James carried on alone, his two

The Transit Telescope at Greenwich Observatory.

This illustration shows the Transit Instrument for observing the times of passage across the Meridian of Greenwich of "clock stars" (standard stars whose positions in the sky are specially well known). These times are used to find the small deviations from perfect time-keeping to which the standard clock may be subject. This standard clock keeps "sidereal time" and it is by comparison of this with the mean solar clock that the mean solar clock is corrected. The Transit Telescope can turn only in the meridian plane.

(CP) A finely graduated silver band which enables the telescope to be correctly set for viewing a clock star.

*'How time – summer and otherwise – is recorded.'*

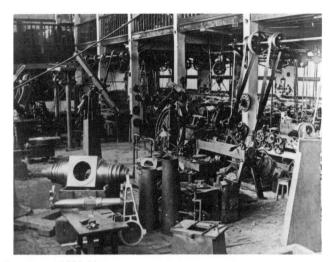

*Charlton Works, interior views, 1880-90.*

sons William, born in 1860, and James, born 1862, being still young. The pattern of production changed little. Transits of the planet Venus across the sun's disc were due in 1874 and 1882. These rare events offered the opportunity for astronomers in widely-separated parts of the globe to time the planet's passage across the sun and by trigonometry to calculate the distance between sun and earth. Numerous expeditions were organised, but Troughton & Simms made only five transits and four portable altazimuths, and refurbished some of the older telescopes that were loaned for the occasion. Descriptions of transits and telescopes built during the later 19th century show that 'hybrids' were common; the structure was often ordered from Grubbs or from Troughton & Simms, but Cooke lenses were specified. Cookes also built domes for other firms' instruments. No doubt the Directors and workmen from these three firms were familiar with each others' factories and well aware of the prosperity or otherwise of their competitors' business.

At Greenwich, Airy was succeeded as Astronomer Royal in 1881 by his former assistant, W. H. M. Christie (1845-1922). Troughton & Simms continued to undertake repairs and perform the annual cleaning of instruments.

The range of theodolites expanded to meet the needs of mineral prospectors and miners. Lightweight metals were increasingly used, since it was estimated in North America that the average mining engineer walked 25 miles per day over rough ground or through mine workings. But aluminium was never as popular in British workshops as it was in America, and for this and other reasons of cost and delivery, American manufacturers began to take over much of the New World market. The interest in mining and minerals did however bring work from the City & Guilds Institute in London, where James collaborated with A. E. Tutton and H. A. Miers to design crystal grinding apparatus, a student's goniometer, and an apparatus to produce monochromatic light for examining crystals.

The Astrophotographic Congress of 1887 held in Paris was the opportunity for Lt A. J. Winterhalter of the Washington Naval Observatory to visit European observatories and manufacturers, that of Troughton & Simms among them. He found Charlton Works, 'still using the time-honoured name of Troughton' flourishing under Simms' management. In the steam-powered factory, nearly 200 men worked to produce a wide range

45

*Equatorial telescope with circles by Edward Troughton refurbished for the Transit of Venus Expedition of 1872, seen in its portable observatory.*

of instruments and apparatus. Winterhalter was impressed by James Simms, describing him as a friendly and open man, entirely without traditional prejudice. Simms' personal attention was essential, particularly as so many instruments were made to the specifications of foreign buyers. Everything needed for the production of precision instruments, from the smallest bolt to high-quality optical work, was made on site. Current output included sextants for the Italian Navy and the Russian government; a new version of the station-pointer which the Royal Navy had chosen in a recent competition, theodolites of a style favoured by the French market, tacheometers for a Spanish customer, and a bewildering variety of other levels and portable transits. Troughton & Simms no longer regularly made large equatorials. There was however a demand for transit circles, with eight-inch aperture telescopes, selling at £1,400, the design and construction of which was now a matter of routine. (Winterhalter saw one such transit circle that had been installed in 1871 when he visited the Austro-Hungarian Hydrographic Department Observatory at Pola, on the Adriatic.) In 1892 Troughton & Simms quoted £1,320 to Christie for a transit of this size for Greenwich. During these years, Troughton & Simms appear to have garnered sufficient business without any great effort on their part. A few catalogues were issued, but the firm seldom participated in trade exhibitions.

Military matters loomed larger before the century closed. The first coincidence rangefinder had been developed by the London instrument maker Patrick Adie in 1860 and now Troughton & Simms worked to improve the patented designs of George Forbes and Arthur Henry Marindin. Forbes' was a rifle rangefinder and after more than a decade of experimentation it was the Zeiss company who finally brought it into production for him. Marindin's was adopted before the First World War as one of the standard infantry rangefinders. During this period, government orders for rangefinders took up much of Troughton & Simms' capacity, sometimes to the detriment of civil orders. (Oddly, coming from a factory reputed for its mechanical

*Charlton Works, building a transit circle.*

abilities, the letters went out in hand-written form until after the war.) James Simms died in 1915, and the business passed to his sons William (1860-1938) and James (1862-1939), who reformed it as a limited liability company. When the war ended, Troughton & Simms found themselves with a backlog of dividing work. (Edward Troughton's dividing engine, fitted with Simms' self-acting device and adapted to run off the factory shafting, was kept in service until the end, though in latter years it did not graduate circles reading to a greater accuracy than one minute of arc.) Yet through-

*Charlton Works, exterior, c1909.*

out the industry, long-term prospects were poor, and it may have been this realisation that prompted the brothers to offer the company to one of their main competitors, T. Cooke & Sons of York, who bought them out in 1922.

———

It is regrettable that the Hydrographic Office archive has been closed during the period of writing this book, limiting evidence for the Charlton Works era to Winterhalter's report and other brief remarks, the census counts and a few photographs. We are thrown back on indirect evidence in the shape of major instruments delivered to observatories in every inhabited continent. Indeed, many survive. Likewise, the number of theodolites, sextants and station pointers in collections or passing through the salerooms suggests an output of thousands, delivered for home and overseas consumption, and this is confirmed by an undated advertisement claiming that 'in fifteen years our output of levels and theodolites alone was 23,000'. Yet without financial returns, in-house reports, publicity or newspaper articles, we cannot assess the scale of the enterprise, the value of turnover, or the impact of the growing factory on the neighbourhood as buildings and railway lines closed in round the site where in the early 1860s a small workshop had been laid out amongst the green fields of rural Charlton.

*Cooke's stand at the London International Exhibition, 1862. Fred and Thomas Cooke junior are seated behind their display of equatorials, a lathe and a turret clock.*

# Part Two – Cooke of York

## Chapter 6: The Self-Made Man – Thomas Cooke of York

THOMAS COOKE'S EARLY LIFE DIFFERED considerably from those of the Troughtons and the Simmses. We have two accounts of his origins, written down after his death, one by his wife and one by his obituarist for the Royal Astronomical Society.

Thomas Cooke was born on 8 March 1807 in the Yorkshire village of Allerthorpe where his father was a shoemaker. Schooled for only two years, he was put to his father's trade, but his imagination was fired by accounts of the exploits of Captain James Cook, and realising that shoemaking was not the road to fortune, he set himself to learn mathematics and navigation in order, as he said, to become a second Captain Cook. At the age of 17, having mastered these subjects, he was ready to depart for the port of Hull, his first step to becoming a famous explorer. At this point his mother begged him not to leave home, and he agreed to stay with her. To give himself an income, he opened a village school, which supported him over the next five years, and it was there that he met Hannah Milner, who later became his wife. From 1829 to 1836 he earned his living schoolmastering and tutoring in York whilst continuing with mathematics and practical mechanics in his leisure hours. At this time he set about making himself a small telescope, grinding one of the lenses from the thick bottom of a glass tumbler and soldering a tin tube for the body of the instrument. This telescope was subsequently bought by John Phillips (1800-74), then Curator of the Yorkshire Museum and soon to be an active force in the British Association for the Advancement of Science, which held its first meeting in York in 1831. Phillips and Cooke enjoyed a warm friendship which continued when Phillips left York to pursue his academic career. Always ready to put in a good word for Cooke's skill, Phillips' influence in the scientific community was invaluable when the young man decided to embark on a full-time career as an optical instrument-maker.

In March 1837, helped by a loan of £100 from his wife's uncle, Cooke leased premises at 50 Stonegate, York. His wife kept the shop (and took in lodgers to make ends meet); Cooke set up his workshop in the rear and prepared to make, repair or retail instruments to order. One of his first tasks was to build his own screw-cutting machine, which served him for many years. Thus equipped, he was ready to undertake his first substantial commission, an equatorial telescope of 4½ inches aperture, for William Gray. The Gray family had an established legal practice in the city of York, and their financial advice and support, again on the basis of family friendship, gave Cooke the practical assistance that he needed to get his business under way.

Gray's telescope was a great success and Cooke regarded it as having made his name as an optician. Indeed, few lenses of this size had been made even in the London workshops. (Unfortunately history does not relate where the glass had been obtained – or if it was an old disc reworked.) In 1851 Cooke made an equatorial telescope with a lens of 7¼ inches aperture – his largest to date – for Hugh Pattinson, a retired metallurgical chemist of Newcastle. Pattinson's friend, Isaac Fletcher, himself a notable astronomer, looked through it and was

# The Cooke Family

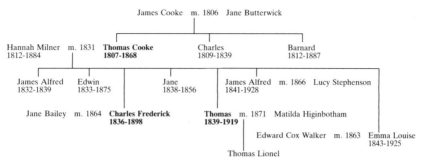

James Cooke   m. 1806   Jane Butterwick

Hannah Milner   m. 1831   **Thomas Cooke**            Charles              Barnard
1812-1884                  **1807-1868**              1809-1839            1812-1887

James Alfred    Edwin              Jane            James Alfred   m. 1866   Lucy Stephenson
1832-1839       1833-1875          1838-1856       1841-1928

Jane Bailey   m. 1864   **Charles Frederick**        **Thomas**   m. 1871   Matilda Higinbotham
                       **1836-1898**                **1839-1919**

                                                   Edward Cox Walker   m. 1863   Emma Louise
                                                                                 1843-1925

                                                   Thomas Lionel

moved to write to Airy proposing that Cooke should be allowed to make the lens for the transit circle to be built for the Cape Observatory. Airy replied that an object glass had already been purchased, but that he would add Fletcher's testimony to the other reports of Cooke's fine work that had already reached him. Cooke's early friendship with (Sir) Norman Lockyer (1836-1920) also paid dividends. Cooke sold Lockyer a telescope in 1861 for his Wimbledon Observatory, and advised him on observing techniques. Lockyer remained a friend of Cooke, bought other equipment from him, and recommended his products whenever possible. Cooke's business did not suffer from being based in York rather than London. Like his contemporary Thomas Grubb of Dublin, Cooke found that the astronomical market for large telescopes was so dispersed that any location with good transport links would serve as a base.

Telescopes brought prestige but there was a steady local demand for spectacles, opera glasses and other small items. In 1849 Cooke advertised his drainage level, a simple device to assist agricultural land managers. By this time he had taken a larger shop in Coney Street, where the 1851 census shows him employing four men and an apprentice – one Lewis Angell, from Clerkenwell, yet more orders flowed in than he could handle. In 1855, leaving his brother Barnard to run the shop, Thomas, with Gray's support, purchased some land at Bishophill, within the York city boundary, where he erected his Buckingham Works. This must have been one of the

earliest scientific instrument manufactories; Cooke made most of his own machine tools and lens-grinding equipment, driven by steam power. There were workshops for brass, glass and wood, and a foundry where all but the largest castings were made.

In 1855 Cooke took the brave step of exhibiting at the Universal Exhibition, held in Paris. His courage certainly paid off, for he was rewarded with the published praises of the Jury, as well as a First Class Medal for his clock-driven equatorial telescope of 7½ inches aperture. Fired, no doubt, by his success, Cooke went on to exhibit regularly at home and abroad. In the summer of 1857 he took a horizontal steam-engine and some surveying instruments, including his drainage level, to the Yorkshire Show. He brought home two First Class Medals from the London Exhibition of 1862, one for the excellent object glasses and mountings of his telescopes, the other for the construction and finish of his turret clock. Cooke had devised an original form of cast iron frame, from which the clock mechanism could be easily withdrawn for repair or adjustment. It boasted a compensated pendulum, to maintain its rate despite changes of temperature. The eminent clockmaker Charles Frodsham, who was the Reporter for the Horological Section, praised Cooke's clocks for the variety of design and their high quality. 'If the pride of high-finished work is destroyed, you can never retain first-rate hands' he wrote with feeling.

*Thomas Cooke (1807-68).*

*Thomas Cooke (1839-1919).*

*Charles Frederick Cooke (1836-98).*

By 1861 the workforce had grown to 26 men – some from London – and 14 boys. Catalogues listed the growing variety of individual eyepieces and mounts, spectacles and opera glasses, hand-held or large clock-driven equatorial telescopes, besides turret clocks, surveying instruments and machine tools. 'The Practical Mechanic's Journal Record of the Great Exhibition' of 1862 spoke highly of the design and execution of all Cooke's exhibits. Their design showed how well Cooke understood kinematics – being nicely balanced and smooth in their motion. For all but the smaller cheaper instruments, he generally mounted the telescope, with its counterbalance and clockwork drive, in the so-called 'German' form of equatorial mount, with its single cast-iron stand. The finest telescopes went to private individuals, a cheaper range being intended for educational use. There were sales to other retailers as far afield as Belfast, Edinburgh and London, for which Cooke was sometimes instructed to engrave the retailer's name, ostensibly as maker. As for his turret clocks, they could be seen on parish church towers, on post offices, factories and schools, and even at Chatsworth, home of the Duke of Devonshire. Their installation involved

Cooke and his workmen in a considerable amount of travelling. One way or another, Cooke was absent from Buckingham Works for much of the time. In 1860 Prince Albert summoned him to Osborne House to discuss the construction of a telescope for the Royal family. The completed instrument, of 5¼ inches aperture, was put on show for 10 days in the window of Cooke's Coney Street shop, before its proud maker escorted it to the Isle of Wight, to be erected for the instruction of the Royal family. There were journeys abroad, to set up telescopes, as well as to attend exhibitions. There was the London end of the business, where Cooke's rented a shop at 31 Southampton Street, Strand, from 1863 till 1869. There were meetings of the Royal Astronomical Society, to which Cooke had been elected in 1859, serving on its Committee in 1865-66. In his absence, Buckingham Works was confided to the care of his sons, Thomas, who had been trained as an optician, and Charles Frederick – always known as Fred – who was a skilled mechanic. It seems probable that Fred was responsible for the steam carriage which Cooke's entered at the 1866 Yorkshire Show.

———

*Cooke's trade cards.*

Into this sunny scene, two storm clouds, as yet no bigger than the proverbial man's hand, arose to wreak havoc on a prosperous business.

Around 1860, Robert Stirling Newall (1812-89), a man grown wealthy from the manufacture of wire rope, had begun negotiations with Cooke for the building of a large telescope. At the 1862 Exhibition, the glassmaking firm of Chance Brothers showed two discs of flint and crown glass, of excellent optical quality and large enough to work into a 25 inch lens – larger than any then in existence. Newall was given first refusal to buy these discs, at £500 each, and he sought quotations from Thomas Grubb of Dublin (an equally reputable maker of large telescopes) and Thomas Cooke, the only two craftsmen capable of handling such large blanks and making the telescope to hold them. Cooke was eager for the contract, but woefully under-estimated the time that he would need to make the lenses and build the telescope. He bid too low and offered a wholly unrealistic delivery date of about one year. Inevitably everything took far longer than expected; he had to make special equipment to handle such large discs, and the concave lens had to be floated on mercury during the grinding process, to prevent it from breaking under its own weight. Years passed before Cooke was satisfied with the lenses, and more years whilst he worked on the telescope itself. Newall grew ever more impatient with what he saw as Cooke's laziness. From time to time he

put in a supervisor, and made token progress payments, but as soon as the supervisor left, work on his telescope ceased. The tone of correspondence between the two men became, on Newall's part, harsh and threatening, on Cooke's part, plaintive. When Newall was about to descend on Buckingham Works, men were pulled off the routine work on which Cooke's livelihood depended, and his cash flow dried up, hence his pleas for weekly payments of £100, to meet his wages bill. Newall even threatened to halt the supply of wire rope which Cooke needed for his turret clocks. In 1867 Cooke's youngest son had the opportunity to buy up his deceased father-in-law's newspaper business in Hull, and Thomas Cooke begged Newall for an advance of £2,000 on account, so that he could assist his son. As the telescope was too large to assemble within Buckingham Works – the length of tube was 32 feet from dew cap to eye end and it weighed nine tons – it was taken into the nearby open space beside the city wall. A special form of driving clock had been designed for it, and was housed in the upper part of the pillar. It was still unfinished at the time of Thomas Cooke's death in 1868.

*Thomas Cooke's steam carriage, c1866.*

What Newall must have known through his contacts in the Royal Astronomical Society, but chose to ignore, was that Cooke was desperately trying to fulfil another large and troublesome order also arising from the 1862 Exhibition.

As mentioned earlier, Troughton & Simms were the principal suppliers to the East India Company and, from 1860, to the government of British India. Lt-Colonel Strange disapproved of this monopoly, but had found no competent alternative supplier when he saw Cooke's stand at the 1862 Exhibition. Impressed by the quality of their workmanship, he immediately took the opportunity to discuss with Cooke the possibility of his supplying the India Office. Nothing loth, Cooke invited Strange to look round Buckingham Works. Strange later wrote of Thomas Cooke, that he was a man of rare genius, who commencing with the humblest possible means had created an optical manufacture vying with, and indeed surpassing, the famed establishments of Germany and France. He was totally devoid of narrow trade conservatism, and ready, unlike most makers, to introduce new forms of construction, provided that they had scientific merit. Strange was influenced by the fact that every part of his instruments was made by Cooke's

own men on his own premises. The same thing, he remarked, could not be said of any other English maker, Troughton & Simms being in 1862 still at Fleet Street. Indeed even when he wrote his report, by which time Charlton Works was operating, Troughton & Simms was less well equipped than Cooke, except in the single matter of dividing.

Strange, aware that Cooke had never built large high-quality surveying instruments and did not undertake precision graduation, took it upon himself to pass the evening hours teaching him the theory and practice of their construction. As Cooke's had no first-rate dividing engine, Thomas Cooke was persuaded to set about building one, every facet of its design being thoroughly discussed by the two men. (How, one wonders, did Thomas Cooke find any time at all to oversee Newall's

*31 Southampton Street, Strand, Cooke's London shop from 1863 to 1869.*

telescope.) In June 1864 Cooke received an order for 16 theodolites of varying sizes, to the value of £368, the first of many such orders for theodolites and levels.

The new self-acting dividing engine had just been completed when Thomas Cooke died on 19 October 1868. He was only 62 but had been ill for some time. His obituarist (could it have been Strange?) writing in *The Athenæum*, grieved for the loss of 'our English Fraunhofer, . . . whose science and skill had restored to England the pre-eminent position she held a century ago in the time of Dollond'. In the confusion following his death, the instruments were delayed, and when they

arrived at Strange's observatory he allowed them to go to India without proper examination. Unfortunately there were complaints; the divisions had been cut on a bevelled azimuth plate and the engine cutter had not scribed cleanly at this angle. Strange was severely reprimanded, and inevitably some of the blame rubbed

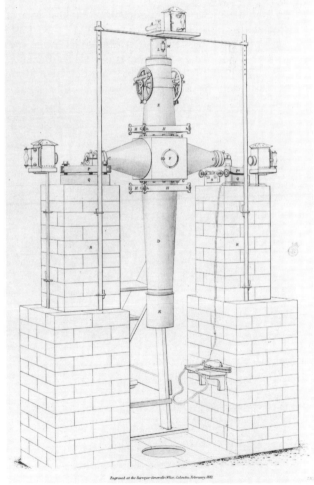

*Large transit by Cooke, 1872, for longitude observations in India. From* Great Trigonometrical Survey, **9**, *(1883); Pl 1.*

off on Cooke's in their hour of general misfortune. Strange returned to York, where he found that Cooke's now had two engines of their own make, plus a third that had been made by Thomas Jones, which they had bought second-hand. Nevertheless he felt it advisable to withhold further theodolite orders until he could be assured of their quality.

Meanwhile, the foundrymen at Buckingham Works wrestled with another order from Strange: two large transits, destined for India. Britain and India had recently been connected by submarine telegraph cable, so it was now possible to measure longitude by making transit observations against Greenwich time signals delivered by telegraph. Strange wished the axes of these transits to be cast from aluminium-bronze, and Cooke's was the only instrument makers able to handle this part of the construction. It took them three years of trial and tribulation. Other problems arose in turn, and were in turn overcome. The transits were shipped to India where they arrived in 1872. The first year's observations were unsatisfactory; transit No. 2 was defective, its joints having been soldered without additional fastening. It was repaired at Madras and after this hiatus the longitude measurements proceeded without further hindrance.

*Cooke turret clock, from* National Encyclopedia, **7**, *(1867-8);*
*'Horology'.*

## TURRET CLOCKS

*Turret clocks are larger than most other clocks and, when they are required to show time on several dials, have an extra train to carry the movement out to the dials. They are powered by a falling weight and the going train is regulated by a pendulum. The striking train is controlled by air pressure acting against a revolving fly. The power needed to drive the striking train, with a heavy hammer to strike the hours, exceeds that of the going train. Cooke's clock as exhibited in the 1862 Exhibition, shown here, was fitted with a gravity remontoire escapement which cut out any irregularities of the wheelwork, by allowing the weight to act directly on the pendulum, giving a smooth and regular movement. Ideally, turret clock dials should be slightly concave and made of slate, stone or cast iron.*

# Chapter 7: Buckingham Works

THOMAS COOKE DIED LEAVING a brief Will bequeathing 'everything' to his wife. This may have included the business, for as his sons laboured to finish Newall's great telescope whilst maintaining production elsewhere in the factory, Newall pressed his claims to the point where, in 1879, he tried to force old Mrs Cooke and her two sons into liquidation. Sir James Meek (1815-91), wealthy industrialist and thrice Lord Mayor of York, rescued the business and then sold it on to James Wigglesworth (1825-1888), who had been a close friend of old Thomas Cooke. (The six-inch refractor that Wigglesworth had bought from Cooke in 1853 served him well for 30 years.) In 1879 Wigglesworth entered into a partnership with Cooke's sons. In his Will, James Wigglesworth offered his son the opportunity to buy Buckingham Works with its house, engines and machinery, for £4,000. Robert Wigglesworth probably did buy Buckingham Works, for he was a partner until the business became a Limited Company in 1897, and thereafter a Director. Meanwhile Newall's telescope had been transferred to his estate at Ferndean near Newcastle in 1870, to be completed in 1871. Newall enjoyed only a brief hour of glory as the owner of the world's biggest refractor for in 1872 the Washington Naval Observatory took delivery of a 28-inch refractor made by the American optician Alvan Clark. Thomas Cooke's reputation lived on: after Newall's death the telescope was transferred to Cambridge University Observatory where his son, Hugh Frank Newall (1857-1944) served as observer, and later Professor of Astrophysics. The lens and the mountings were of such

*Building the Newall telescope, c1870.*

excellent quality that it was used at Cambridge until the 1950s, and thereafter at the Greek National Observatory in Athens.

Thomas Cooke's sons had circulated their customers, assuring them that high standards would be maintained, and this does seem to have been the case. A batch of levels sent out to the Survey of India in 1870 met with complaints over the way in which the tripods had been constructed. The matter was put right without needing to return them, and the reports written at the time stress the high quality of workmanship. Cooke's former craftsman, Richard Wehlisch (c1838-1904), now in charge of the Mathematical Instrument Workshop at Calcutta, wrote 'The levels in question are in every respect some of the best ever imported, with all the latest improvements'. This opinion was echoed by his Superintendant, Colonel Gastrell, who referred to 'The excellence of the workmanship and form of Messrs Cooke & Co's levels . . .'. The Survey of India Reports show that Cooke's replaced Troughton & Simms at this time, as supplier of levels for the primary survey. Cooke's enjoyed a high standing within the trade, attracting apprentices and improvers from London and overseas, men who were subsequently proud to attest to their training in York. H. W. Vallé, who set up in business in Brisbane, and Christian Louis Berger (b1842), son of the Court Armourer of Wurttemberg, who established his own manufactory in Boston, had both served time with Cooke's and other major instrument makers. George L. Buff, who had worked at York before crossing the Atlantic in 1864 to establish himself in Boston, was probably also a former Cooke's employee.

———

Around 1884 work began on a major engineering project closer to home: the Forth Bridge, which would carry the railway line north from Edinburgh. Detailed surveys of the area were undertaken, using as principal instrument a 12-inch theodolite by Cooke, fitted with a small downward-pointing telescope to substitute for a plumb-bob. R. E. Middleton, one of the engineers concerned, was responsible for this and other modifications to the smaller theodolites, whereby they served to align the structure as building progressed. For this purpose, Cooke's fitted a reflector to the object-glass end of an ordinary type of theodolite. This reflector was carried by a sleeve and graduated limb, from which the reflected angle of line-of-sight could be measured. Middleton declared the Cooke instruments excellent, and 'practically indestructible'. The bridge was opened in 1890 and recently celebrated its centenary.

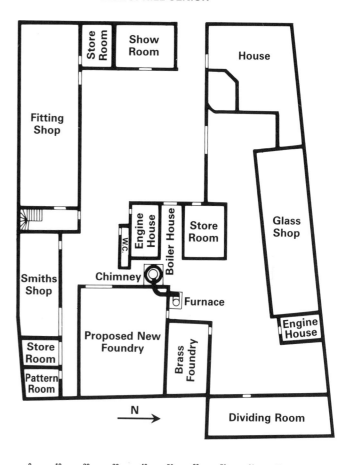

*Plan of Buckingham Works, 1871.*

Equatorial telescopes continued to be a mainstay of business. Cooke's supplied the growing number of important domestic observatories, as well as many of the 'second-generation' observatories, now under construction in the colonies and dependencies. Frederick also undertook the construction of domes, and is said to have

*Surveyors and their apparatus, Forth Bridge survey, 1885.*

been the first to substitute papier-mâché panels (as customarily used by carriage makers) for the heavier copper cladding formerly employed. These domes were prefabricated at York, then dismantled and shipped out for re-erection on site by Cooke's men. This required considerable skill in design and construction, if everything was to match up at the destination. In 1883 Cooke's obtained an order for a dome at Greenwich, with a bid that undercut Thomas Grubb. In 1884 James Wigglesworth built himself a new observatory at

Scarborough for which Cookes supplied a fine 15½-inch telescope and a dome with papier-mâché panels and a sliding shutter of their own design. The dome was much admired, for the quietness of its rotation and its steadiness in high winds. In 1893, the Astronomer Royal William Christie fitted a new large telescope on an existing mount, for which Cooke's built an onion-shaped dome, the only shape which would allow the telescope to rotate. Frederick based his design on a dome previously made for William Lassell; the work took six months and

*Assembling Cookes' dome, Cape of Good Hope, c1896.*

*Cookes' dome, Cape of Good Hope, 1896.*

the result met with general satisfaction. Unlike some cheaper domes which turned on rolling cannon-balls, it had large wheels travelling on a flat rail, which reduced friction to a minimum. By the end of the century, Cooke domes could be seen at the Cape – David Gill reported that his Cooke dome was 'an admirable piece of work and I think the best dome in the world' – Brussels, Sofia, Odessa, Rio de Janeiro, Liège, Teramo, and Madras.

Overseas, Cooke telescopes could be found in Adelaide, from where observations of the Transit of Venus were made in 1874 and 1882; at the new observatory of Uccle, outside Brussels, built in 1889 (a Cooke mount with a Merz lens and a Breguet clock); Liège University, built in 1881, which had a 10-inch equatorial; Copenhagen, Glasgow, Madras, Poona, Cadiz, Sydney, and Trieste, among others. The telescope ordered for the Brazilian National Observatory at a cost of £2,000 had a sad history. Delivered in 1894, it was

*Cookes' dome, Greenwich Observatory, c1892.*

photographic use, it had to have interchangeable eyepieces. Cooke's supplied the heliometers, spectroscopes, driving clocks, micrometers, and other fittings which made up the well-furnished observatory. A profitable line of business was the refurbishment of old telescopes, which were bought in on the death of their previous owner, or accepted in part exchange for a new instrument. Not all sales went through smoothly. A 10-inch equatorial being built in 1871 for the Japanese Government was left on Cookes' hands and was later sold at Stevens auction rooms for £700 to the telegraph magnate W. T. Henley. The spectroscope prisms made for Charles Piazzi Smyth at Edinburgh did not satisfy and he turned instead to the firm of Adam Hilger, who were already masters of this art.

Catalogues issued during this era illustrate Cookes' wide range of manufactures. Small telescopes, binoculars, microscopes and other optical goods, surveying, telegraphic and electrical instruments, steam engines, machine tools, and a pneumatic despatch system (these were pipes installed in large offices to 'pump' documents or packets round the building), all testify to an expanding market for precision apparatus. Besides their private customers, Cooke's supplied the Admiralty, War Office, Board of Works, Post Office, various railway companies and military colleges. Exhibitions were still a useful means of getting publicity. At the London Exhibition of 1871 Cooke's showed equatorial telescopes with four-inch and 10-inch object glasses, a 14-inch Everest theodolite and a five-inch War Department theodolite, a six-inch transit, two levels, and an electric motor clock driving eight dials. Much the same collection was sent to the Vienna Exhibition of 1873.

intended for a planned new observatory which was delayed for 20 years during which time this telescope and other instruments rusted and decayed in their crates.

Celestial photography, which had begun in a small way in the 1840s, became more important as photographic processes improved. For this work, modified telescope lenses were needed, as the wavelengths which gave the best photograph differed from those best seen by the human eye. Unless the telescope was dedicated to

Whatever the financial damage caused by the Newall telescope, and perhaps other under-estimated contracts, it is clear that by the 1880s Cooke's were having difficulty in meeting their operating costs. In 1891 the bank refused to increase its overdraft to enable them to purchase more property, and in 1893 this overdraft had risen above £6,000. By 1894 the weekly wages bill was

£200, and at one point a special authorisation had to be given to add this modest sum to the overdraft. These problems were probably a reflection of the general malaise affecting British industry during the last quarter of the 19th century and the early years of the new century. In 1884-86 a Royal Commission on the Depression of Trade and Industry published its Report in three large volumes, and although neither Cooke's nor York was specifically mentioned, we may suppose that precision engineering and scientific instrument manufacturing suffered along with the industries that they served. Britain was undergoing a second industrial revolution, but lagged behind Germany and the United States where technology and industrial organisation were being vigorously pursued. This revolution was characterised by a new era of precision machining performed on automatic lathes and screw-cutting machines, powered by small electric motors which allowed each workman to run his machine at its optimum power for the job in hand, a facility not available in the old belt-driven workshops where the speed of working was imposed at the central power source. Labour direction and supervision improved, with wage incentives being given for speed and quality of production. But most of these revolutionary techniques were imported, and Britain still lacked the training facilities and the means to involve scientists in the world of manufacturing industry which were clearly beneficial to Germany and the United States. The British voices urging change were ignored by industrialists and government alike.

Despite this national gloom, Buckingham Works grew steadily by a process of infill and the acquisition of adjacent houses. A description of the Works in 1894, shortly before further enlargement, explained how Cooke's large-scale optical work had led to increasing emphasis on precision heavy engineering. 'With the exception of the actual making of the glass, the whole construction of a telescope is carried out at their works, even the heavy cast-iron pillars being made in their own foundry. This, no doubt, is partly due to the fact that this firm have never confined themselves to telescope work only, but have also made large quantities of high-class lathes and machine tools, and other machines where especially accurate workmanship is required. An essential to the successful working of such tools is that the framing shall be heavier than is required for mere strength, hence this has led to the development of the foundry department, so that now castings of considerable size are produced and machined in the ordinary course of business. . . . The works of the firm cover 23,000 square feet of ground, including a large and lofty erecting shop, measuring 77 feet by 76 feet. The metal-working shops are kept distinct from those for glass-working, and consist of a group of buildings three stories high. On the ground floor are the brass and iron foundries, and all the heavier tools . . . including a large gear-cutting machine, which is capable of taking blanks 6½ feet in diameter. The large dividing engine is also fixed on this floor to ensure steadiness, but is in a room apart by itself and is erected on an insulated masonry pier sunk some depth below ground level. With this engine circles 58 inches in diameter can be divided. The upper floors contain the lighter lathes, milling machines and engraving machines. . . . The pattern and wood-working shop is at the top of this building, and large quantities of well-seasoned mahogany are always stored, from which the legs for theodolite and level tripods are prepared. The works are lit by electricity, which is generated on the premises.' Sketches of the Works show the chimney of the steam-engine which was the power source.

To the journal *Engineering*, Cooke's were precision engineers *par excellence*. A long article in 1894 detailed their recent achievements. There was a length-comparator made for van den Kerchove of Ghent. A large and solid structure, it could measure bars up to eight feet long, to an accuracy of $\frac{1}{20,000}$ inch. It had been made to such fine tolerances that Cookes' engineers had been troubled by the slight expansion of the machine bed on warm days. Another product still in demand was the pneumatic despatch system, which was now in service in numerous government and private institutions. Cookes' panto-

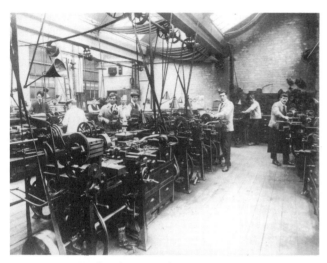

*Buckingham Works, interior view.*

*Buckingham Works, showing a coudé telescope under construction.*

graph had been developed for their own use from a design that Lt-Colonel Strange had suggested to old Thomas Cooke. Cooke's used it to letter their circles, and for general engraving work, and would build one for anyone else who cared to buy it.

————

The latter part of the 19th century witnessed the discovery and exploitation of the South African gold fields, stimulating a demand for surveying instruments from that quarter. Small amounts of gold had been exported for centuries but in 1854 deposits were discovered near the site of the future city of Johannesburg. Between 1864 and 1870 Carl Mauch, a German prospector, explored north of the Transvaal and into the land between the Limpopo and Zambesi rivers, returning to prophesy that enormous wealth would be found there. The gold deposits lay in ancient river-delta fans, buried deep beneath later sediments, and these 'blanket beds' could be followed from their outcrops. Reef mining began in Transvaal in 1872 and the first successful deep mine there was opened in 1873. The gold fever

which followed the discovery of the Sheba reef in 1886 was short-lived; but it triggered a general interest in prospecting and mining across a wide area. So promising were the mines surrounding the straggle of shanties known as Johannesburg that a town was laid out in 1886 and subsequently grew into the largest city in southern Africa.

Cooke's responded to the demand for instruments by opening a branch at 37 Castle Street, Cape Town, in 1899. It stocked a full range of Cooke's own surveying and drawing instruments, also Chesterman rules and tapes, and Zeiss microscopes. In an adjacent workshop, staff trained at York had the appropriate machinery to undertake repairs. The cost of shipping raised the prices in South Africa considerably above those at home; a four-inch theodolite, priced £28 at York, cost £33 at Cape Town and £42-10-0 at Johannesburg. A 20-inch Cooke level priced at £25 at York sold for £57 at Cape Town, and a four-inch compass, price £4 at York, cost £4-15-0 at Cape Town and £7 at Johannesburg. At Johannesburg and further afield, Cooke's relied on

*Buckingham Works, 1906, telescope for Sir Thomas Sebastian Bazley.*

Before the end of the century, Cooke's, like its competitors, began to supply what were known as 'optical munitions'; that is, rangefinders, gun and rifle sights, and surveying and engineering instruments adapted to military needs. Science and technology had begun to make their mark in the American Civil War of 1861, and later in the Franco-Prussian War. However, whilst France and Germany appointed scientists to their military committees, Britain remained largely complacent. No year of Queen Victoria's reign had been free of war, but these were petty colonial affairs, fought against unsophisticated tribesmen, and put down by sending a small expeditionary force or a couple of gunboats. In 1899 the government believed that it could silence the rebellious Boer farmers within a year, at a cost of £10 million. In the event, the Boer War lasted until 1902, cost some £250 million, and was declared to have been a 'Great War'. More munitions were called for than were available. The Ordnance factories had no hope of meeting demand, and the private armament firms such as Armstrongs and Vickers were prevailed on to promise far more than they could achieve. Had there been any naval involvement, disaster would have been assured. As it was, the demand was for artillery weapons, and optical munitions formed a part of these.

It was not a case of starting entirely from scratch; 'War Department' theodolites were shown at the 1871 Exhibition, as mentioned earlier and in 1887 Cooke had filed a patent in connection with gunsights. The Watkin Artillery Position-Finder was another such item. In 1888 Major H. S. S. Watkin RA received £25,000 from the government in exchange for transferring his patents to the War Office, and Cooke's manufactured it under a cloak of secrecy. It was in fact a depression rangefinder, weighing about one ton, and requiring some very accurate gear-cutting. Watkin was also responsible for the Mekometer, a lightweight rangefinder for cavalry and infantry use. This consisted of two instruments resembling box sextants separated by a cord of fixed length – usually 50 yards. A right-angle triangle was set up between the observers and the distant object to be

agencies, but this was something of a mixed blessing since agents generally dealt in instruments from several manufacturers and could not be relied on to give preference to Cooke instruments.

A London office seems to have been less important. The shop in Southampton Street had been vacated in 1869, and Cooke's had no London base until they leased premises in Victoria Street in 1895.

———

*The Watkin Mekometer.*

*Alfred Taylor (1863-1940).*

ranged and the third angle read off in terms of distance. Cooke's also made the Grenfell gunsight, to the design of the naval gunnery expert H. H. Grenfell (1845-1906). To market these sensitive military instruments, an agreement was drawn up in 1896 (and renewed in 1898) between H. H. Grenfell Ltd, H. S. S. Watkin, T. Cooke & Sons Ltd and Vickers, whereby Cooke's manufactured optical munitions for Vickers' contracts.

With so many firms in Britain and particularly in Germany active in the same field, all new and potentially valuable ideas were covered by patents. Further, from 1891 Cooke's advertised their willingness to assist inventors in bringing their designs to a practical form. The patents filed by Frederick and Thomas Cooke indicate the scope of the firm's interests. They include railway signalling apparatus, 1867; engineers' levels, 1884; electric arc lamps, 1885; pneumatic despatch systems, 1885-6; and the gunsights mentioned earlier. Patents filed by surveyors working overseas included the reversible levels of Thomas Bolton, of the India Department, 1893, and the 'percentage theodolite' devised by James Fergusson of Vancouver, 1898. The Bolton and Fergusson instruments were made and marketed by Cooke's for a number of years. In 1898 J. Bridges-Lee licenced Cooke's to manufacture his photo-theodolite for a period of five years. Licences were taken on overseas patents: in their 1896 catalogue Cooke's advertised the Ziegler Tacheograph which had been patented in Luxemburg by Ziegler and Hager. For their own workshops, Cooke's bought the English rights to the van Hoesen & Wilson bubble-tube grinding machine, an American invention, which was patented in Britain in 1897. A reversible level, designed in 1879 but not patented, by Thomas Cushing, Inspector of Scientific Instruments at the India Office, was supplied to the Survey of India from 1880.

———

Old Thomas Cooke's widow Hannah died in 1884. In 1894 Frederick retired from the business in favour of Alfred Taylor (1863-1940), and in 1897 the firm was reformed as a limited liability company. The management of the optical side of the business had already been handed over to Harold Dennis Taylor (1862-1943) (no relation to Alfred Taylor).

Dennis Taylor had been educated at St Peter's School, York, and was training to become an architect when he was offered employment at Thomas Cooke's. At the time of his arrival, optical design was, as it had been since the days of Thomas Cooke senior, a matter of trial and error based on experience and practice, with only a token nod to theoretical formulae. There were no textbooks or training courses available and Taylor set about learning what he could from the voluminous writings of G. B. Airy, as developed by Professor Henry Coddington. A brilliant and inventive young man, Taylor made good use of this difficult material and in 1883, soon after his arrival, he filed his first patent for a photographic exposure meter. He followed this by others for a new type of astronomical lens, and for what became known as the 'Cooke photographic lens' which did away with first-order aberration, a previously unavoidable distortion of the image. These were the first of some 50 patents relating to all classes of optical instruments, plus sundry other ideas that came to his mind. Cooke's took advantage of these patents in different ways, buying some outright from Taylor and paying him royalties on others. In 1891 Taylor published his book, *The Adjustment and Testing of Telescope Objectives*, which immediately became the established authority in its field. It was translated into German, reissued in 1896 and 1921, expanded in 1946 and reprinted in 1983. Taylor was the first to use star collimation to test the performance of telescopes, a method which became general practice for many years. The 'Cooke photographic lens' (a loose term whose interpretation was to cause difficulties in later years) was a three-element lens which gave remarkable flatness of field. It could be used in telescopes as well as in portrait cameras and it soon generated such demand that Cooke's licenced its manufacture to the optical firm of Taylor, Taylor & Hobson of Leicester. (The Taylor brothers were unrelated to either of the Taylor's at Buckingham Works.) In 1895 Cooke lenses received the Royal Photographic Society's medal for meritorious inventions. For many years they were the basis for practically every photographic lens, being superior to the German lenses at this time.

In 1893 Dennis Taylor was appointed Optical Manager and this was followed in 1895 by a seat on the Board of Directors. For the next 20 years he devoted himself to the improvement of optical processes and the development of new machinery and testing equipment. About 1895 he went to the Schott glassworks at Jena, in order to ensure a supply of certain optical glass then only made in Germany, where he met Professor Ernst Abbe, who did so much to develop the German optical industry.

Towards the end of the last century, the large refractor telescope was still regarded as the prime instrument for an observatory, yet even the best so-called 'achromatic' lenses gave a coloured fringe. Experienced astronomers simply ignored this effect but it certainly lowered the quality of photographic and spectrographic images. In Germany and England optical glass manufacturers experimented with new mixes, but it became evident that no two-element lens would give a truly colourless field. The winner in this race for perfection was Dennis Taylor, who in 1892 achieved an achromatic lens made up of three elements, including a new glass from the Schott Works at Jena. It was of course patented in Britain, and shortly afterwards, in France and the USA. Telescopes constructed to this design, the first 'triple apochromats', met with great success. Their colour correction was so good, and was so successfully combined with the other five corrections needed, that they could be used for both photographic and visual work, and are correctly described as 'photo-visual objectives'. Taylor's design limited the practical size of the lens, and it still gave a distorted image unless it was perfectly centered in its cell. Consequently there had to be some means of restraining the lens as its cell expanded in warm weather. The brilliantly simple mechanical solution was probably Frederick's contribution. The cell was fitted with zinc strips and bronze wedges, able to slide over one another. Zinc expands more than bronze when the temperature rises, so that as the cell wall expanded, the inner strips and wedges kept the lens truly central.

During the winter of 1897-98 Taylor was asked by John Franklin-Adams (1843-1912) to design a six-inch

*Buckingham Works, arrangement for photographing the Franklin-Adams telescope, c1900.*

short-focus lens with good definition over a wide field, for celestial photography. In the autumn of 1898 the lens was temporarily mounted and employed for one year at Franklin-Adams' observatory in Argyllshire. Taylor examined the photos that had been taken, and recomputed his figures. A new four-inch lens was built, with the intention to refigure the original six-inch if the new lens was satisfactory. The telescope went to Spain for the 1900 eclipse and took such good photographs that the six-inch was refigured, then a 10-inch made. In its brass and aluminium cell this lens weighed about 180 lbs. Franklin-Adams designed his own variation on an English mounting and made a full-size schematic model for Cooke's to develop. The mount was designed to carry two cameras with lenses of unequal sizes, to be used simultaneously. Its axis ran in double ball-bearings which was Cooke's common practice for their larger telescopes. The telescope was erected at Cape Town where it performed so well that Franklin-Adams asked for a duplicate but was told that 'alas the melting from which my discs had been made had all been used and another melting could not be depended on to give the same focus and therefore the same scale'. His words reveal that the manufacture of optical glass was still a very inexact science.

Many years later, when awarding Taylor the Physical Society's Duddell Medal, Professor Rankine alluded to this early work, remarking on the beauty of design ultimately reached. The specifications of the lenses were notable documents of high scientific value in their own right, and by 1934, at the time of the award, four official editions of them had appeared, the last nearly 40 years after the patent was granted. In the specifications of the Cooke lenses nothing was more striking than Taylor's handling of the theory which enabled him to achieve his aims. Were further tribute needed, Rankine would point to the way that others, particularly in Germany, had imitated Taylor immediately his patents expired. Meanwhile, at the close of the 19th century, the patents were still valid and Taylor was doing his best to carry Cooke's forward into a bright technological future.

*Cooke equatorial telescope made for Negretti & Zambra, c1920.*

# Chapter 8: Changing Horizons – Changing Output

BUCKINGHAM WORKS, AS THE 20th century dawned, consisted of several three-storey buildings extending from Bishophill Senior to Albion Street. A 20hp Crossley gas engine was installed as the main power source. A foundry, glass and metal workshops, the bubble-tube grinding and dividing engines, wood and leather workshops, made the firm almost self-sufficient. Only one vital element – optical glass – was largely imported, from Germany.

The overseas market for surveying instruments remained buoyant. In 1902 Cooke's opened an office at Fort Winnipeg in Canada, and in the same year they negotiated with a Canadian surveyor, J. C. Fergusson, to make and sell his 'percentage theodolite'. Its circle was divided half in conventional degrees and half to a formula that, by solving trigonometrical problems by simple arithmetic, allowed it to act as a rangefinder. The old drainage and Bolton levels were abandoned, and a new class of instrument, the Cooke unifilar magnetometer, appeared in the catalogues.

This magnetometer had been designed by H. A. Denholm Fraser, to serve the Magnetic Survey of India, which began operations in 1900. It differed from existing models in its lighter and more robust construction. Aluminium cells reduced its overall weight. Its scales were engraved on optical glass, in place of the photographic scale in Kew magnetometers, and the silk suspension for the magnet was replaced by a phosphor-bronze ribbon.

Six of these instruments went to India, along with spare parts in case of accidents in the field and with the principal components made to gauge so as to be interchangeable in different instruments. '. . . the new unifilars have been made with very great care by Messrs Cooke & Sons, and have shown themselves in certain respects to be an improvement on the present pattern Kew instruments, at all events for work in the field' was Denholm Fraser's comment. These same magnetometers were adopted by the US Coast Survey, and in due course found their way to Canada and South America. By the 1920s an all-purpose version with azimuth circle was on offer.

Six lightweight theodolites were constructed from a special gunmetal and aluminium and adapted for sub-zero conditions, and an old Troughton & Simms transit was overhauled, for the British Antarctic (*Terra Nova*) Expedition of 1910-13. The dramatic circumstances surrounding this expedition, which turned into a race for the Pole, followed by the death of Scott and his companions on the homeward trek, bestowed a certain publicity value on the instruments, which were featured in Cookes' advertising material for many years.

Astronomical apparatus still figured on the order book. A second telescope was ordered for Rio, and was sent out in 1909 to join the earlier one in store. A third telescope was delivered in 1923, when the new observatory was finally being laid out. This was the last to be built at Buckingham Works before the amalgamation with Troughton & Simms. It received exhaustive coverage in the journal *Engineering*, and was indeed a masterpiece of complexity. At its heart was an 18-inch refractor, with completed the equipment. This dome with its iron frame and papier-mâché panels weighed 10 tons, yet a pull on the hand-ropes sufficed to set it rolling.

World-wide, orders came in for Dennis Taylor's new photographic objectives. He modified the Cooke lens of 1893, patenting improvements in 1905 and 1906. In 1904 he discovered by chance that light transmission through optical glass was increased by a tarnished or bloomed surface, and this happy discovery was turned to good account as the basis of a standard manufacturing process. In 1906 he published *A System of Applied Optics* which developed Coddington's work into a complete system of formulae for optical design. Many other optical designers were guided and inspired by this book, which ran through editions in English and

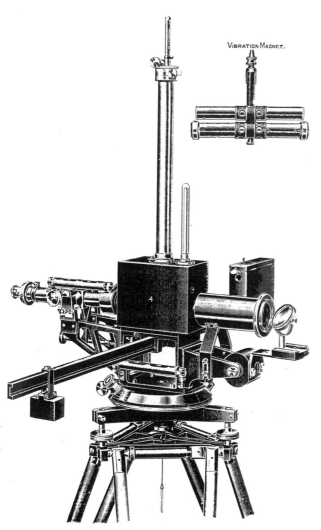

*Cooke magnetometer, 1901.*

*Cooke portable transit telescope, made for the Presidency College, Calcutta, 1904.*

a 10-inch following telescope and a 5-inch finder. Two astrophotographic cameras of 10 inches aperture were supported on the same mounting. A 33-feet diameter dome with double shutter and special observing ladder

*Lightweight theodolite made by Cookes for the 1912 (Terra Nova) Antarctic Expedition.*

*Dennis Taylor (1861-1943).*

German. In 1907 he was responsible for the 'optical square' arrangement, which was applied to rangefinders. He contributed articles to the *Monthly Notices of the Royal Astronomical Society* and to other journals dealing with optical matters. In 1923, long after his formal retirement, he received the Royal Photographic Society's Traill Taylor Medal, and gave the associated Memorial Lecture, in 1933 the Society further rewarded him with its Progress Medal. In 1934 he received the Duddell Medal of the Physical Society, 'for contributions to the advancement of knowledge by the invention and design of scientific instruments'. Dennis Taylor married Charlotte Barff, and they had a daughter and two sons, one of whom, Wilfred, said of him, 'My father was a man of encyclopaedic knowledge, who always seemed to be working out some new optical invention or formula. He could, none the less, put all this to one side and derive great pleasure from a country walk, cycle ride, or climb. His tastes were simple and he was very self-sufficient. My mother understood him well and knew how to order the household so as to give his genius full scope.' He counted gardening, astronomy, photography and natural history among his hobbies, and spent his retirement years in the Yorkshire village of Coxwold.

———

*Buckingham Works, building the telescope for the Brazilian National Observatory, c1894.*

*The Brazilian telescope in its Cooke dome, Rio de Janeiro.*

As the drums of war continued to roll, the maritime nations embarked on a re-armament programme. The great capital ships and fast cruisers presented new problems in long-range naval gunnery. Guns now had a range of several miles, too far to estimate by eye, particularly when the enemy vessel was obscured by smoke, shell-splash or simple bad weather. If, however, a sequence of ranges and bearings of the target ship could be observed, the change-of-range rate (that is,

how fast the two ships were converging or moving apart) could be calculated and the guns aimed ahead of the moving target. In 1902 Lt J. S. Dumaresq devised a trigonometrical slide-rule calculator which combined the courses, speeds and bearings of firing ship and target to estimate the change-of-range rate. In 1904 the Admiralty experimented with a mechanical device that generated ranges independently of observations. This machine, which had been developed by Vickers, consisted of a clockwork motor, set to run at a speed corresponding to the change-of-range rate between the two ships, driving a pointer round a dial marked in ranges, hence its name: the Vickers clock. The machine took the calculations a stage further, but left a certain amount of guesswork in the system. It was to eliminate this uncertainty factor that a civilian inventor, Arthur Pollen, became involved with the Admiralty, and with Cooke's.

Arthur Joseph Hungerford Pollen (1866-1937), trained as a barrister, was Managing Director of the Linotype company at the beginning of the century. From the time of the Boer War he became obsessed with the idea of devising a method whereby naval guns could be fired with a similar accuracy to those of the artillery. The elements of Pollen's 'A.C. System' (the initials stood for Aim Correction) were a rangefinder, a 'clock' and a plotting-table, all of which went through various stages of development. To begin with, he teamed up with Harold Isherwood, a Linotype engineer. The mechanical parts were built at the Linotype factory, the telescope units bought from Cooke's. By September 1905 Pollen's observing and plotting instruments were ready for trial. The apparatus consisted of a rangefinder from which simultaneous transmissions of range and bearings were mechanically integrated by the clock to show the future speed and course of the enemy ship. A gyroscope control isolated the system from errors of aim due to yaw of the firing ship.

In 1908 Pollen set up the Argo Company to hold his patents and handle the business of manufacturing and selling his system. This was easier said than done. Pollen met the inevitable prejudice from supporters of other systems, and also from certain greybeards in the Admiralty, some of whom were convinced that the situation that his system handled most successfully – where the attack and target ships were converging fast – would never happen. A series of bruising encounters with a succession of Admiralty and Ordnance staff was exacerbated by Pollen's habit of circulating printed diatribes whenever he felt that he had suffered some injustice. Nor did his familiarity with politicians,

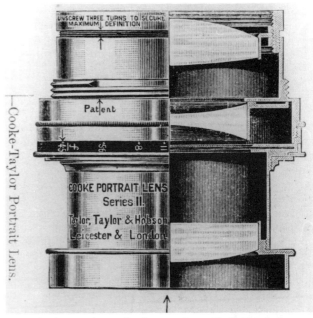

*Cooke lens with iris diaphragm, from T. Cooke & Sons,* Astronomical Instruments *Catalogue, 1908.*

businessmen and journalists endear him to naval men. When he was on the brink of selling some part of his apparatus, he more than once lost the order through demanding too high a price for his development costs. The story is long and involved, parts of it masked by military secrecy. There is room here only to explain Pollen's relationship with Cooke's.

At the same time that Pollen was developing his system, the Admiralty advertised for a rangefinder capable of measuring ranges up to 5½ miles. In response to this advertisement, Cooke's submitted a 10-foot base, single-observer, rangefinder to the Admiralty in 1906. Until then, such long bases were impossible to make because the metal reflectors had to be housed within an absolutely rigid base tube. In Cookes' rangefinder the mirrors were replaced by pentagonal prisms whose surfaces of reflection cancelled out minor shifts of alignment. Consequently, very-long-base rangefinders became feasible, because their slight flexure did not spoil the observation. On this occasion, however, the Admiralty's choice fell on a rangefinder made by Barr & Stroud of Glasgow.

In 1908 the Linotype Company moved its base of operations to America, leaving Pollen without workshop facilities. When in June 1910 he received £15,000 advance payment on the Admiralty order for mountings and range-and-bearing indicators, he immediately bought shares in Cooke's, which gave him a seat on the Board and access to their skilled optical and precision engineers. In 1910-11 Pollen and Taylor collaborated on a novel rangefinder which would work in dim light. The conventional optical system of double telescope and prisms was replaced by a single wide-aperture telescope and plane mirrors, giving an eight-fold brightness of image. Much later this Cooke-Pollen rangefinder achieved a certain success in postwar naval trials. Smaller instruments were also required by the Navy: in 1914 Cooke's signed an agreement with Admiral A. W. Waymouth (1863-1936) for a hand-held rangefinder to his pattern, which went through a series of modifications over the years.

By 1911 the military potential of the improved A.C. System led the Admiralty to move in and supress certain

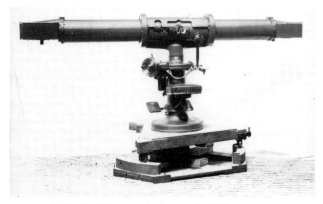

*Pollen's AC rangefinder, early 20th century.*

patents, paying £3,660 for Pollen's services and a pledge to secrecy. This allowed the Admiralty to commission 'mixed' apparatus, with elements from several inventors combined into a single system. Throughout the pre-war years, Pollen was competing against the Dreyer fire control apparatus, which was mechanically inferior to his own, but simpler to understand and maintain, and available to the Admiralty at a far lower cost. It was being made by Elliott Brothers, whose engineer, and later Director, (Sir) Keith Elphinstone, was a frequent visitor to York. In October 1911 Elphinstone examined the Argo Mk III clock then under construction and all the drawings, presumably with a view to constructing one of these 'mixed' systems. Pollen took a lease on Bishophill House in 1912, where his own designers and engineers could be close to Buckingham Works.

At this stage the Admiralty lost interest in the A.C. System and terminated its monopoly contract with Pollen. Within six months Argo was selling all Cooke's could make to foreign buyers, the arrangement being that Cooke's manufactured on a fixed-profit basis. The Argo Company's lack of capital, which hampered its preparations to sell abroad, appears to have been eased in mid-1913 by a new share issue amounting to £25,000, of which a certain proportion was taken up by Cooke's in partial payment for goods manufactured. The Argo Company began its sales campaign in September, probably having in stock at this time three Argo Clocks Mk IV, three Pollen-Cooke rangefinders with improved mountings, and one helm-free true course plotting-table, all of which had been ordered from Cooke & Sons in late 1912, in addition to the five Argo Clocks destined for the Royal Navy. By the summer of 1914, Argo had reached agreements with Russia and Austro-Hungary. Negotiations with Brazil and Chile were nearly concluded, discussions were underway with USA, whilst Turkey, Greece, Italy and France were all showing interest. Now Pollen was faced with needing to expand Cookes' manufacturing capacity to meet his demand at a time when space, tools and manpower were in short supply.

The outbreak of war placed the Argo Company in a precarious position with regard to its foreign sales. The Austro-Hungarian order lapsed because of hostilities between the two nations. The Russian order was complicated by the closure of the Baltic to British shipping. The Americans suspended discussions for a variety of reasons – not least, Pollen's high prices and the fact that the American Sperry Company was developing a home-grown predictor. The Admiralty took over the Chilean battleship then nearing completion and Brazil, for financial reasons, cancelled its order for the battleship that Vickers was to have built. Faced by this abrupt loss of business, Pollen tried to sell his stock-in-hand to the Royal Navy, but met with no interest. He then completed the Russian order, now reduced to three rangefinders with indicators, two Mk V Clocks, and two gyroscopes, and despatched it in October 1914. The Argo Company was closed down, and by the spring of 1915 Pollen had become a full-time war journalist. It seems unlikely that Cooke's profited from their association with Argo.

In 1915 Vickers acquired a 70% holding in Cooke's, to satisfy their requirements for optics in ordnance work, and to get control of the Pollen apparatus. Cooke's were also making Vickers-designed anti-aircraft predictors and the Vickers clock mentioned above. After the war, Cooke's made the Argo designs to Vickers' instructions and this became known as the Spanish Coast Defence Gear. In 1926 the Royal Commission on Awards to Inventors paid Pollen £30,000 for his fire control apparatus.

The British government failed to learn from its experience in the Boer War that no armaments industry could immediately step up production unless it was subsidised to keep spare capacity in peacetime. Consequently, on the outbreak of war, the Royal Ordnance factories could not hope to meet demand, and the private armaments suppliers, Armstrongs, Vickers, and others, lacked reserves of workshops or skilled manpower on which to draw. Again, these companies were pressured into making unrealistic forecasts of production,

*Women working in Cookes' factory during World War I.*

which again they failed to meet. Eventually in 1915 a Ministry of Munitions was created, with optical munitions within its remit. Some of the companies concerned (apparently not including Cooke's) set up the British Optical Manufacturers' Association to negotiate on their behalf. The Ministry discovered that the optical industry was accustomed to buy its glass from overseas, and set about coaxing and compelling Messrs Chance to modernise and vastly increase its output. The optical manufacturers were condemned as conservative in their ways, and they too had to be propelled into the modern age by accepting increased mechanisation and a 'dilution' of the workforce with unskilled men, boys, and women. Grumbling, no doubt, about the additional facilities that would be required, this was done, and production rose to a satisfactory level.

Cooke's increased their manufacturing capacity still further by taking over adjacent houses. Heating and ventilation was installed in the factory. There was a dining hall for 300 men. A new foundry to cast brass and aluminium was built, with a pattern-store protected against the risk of fire. The Ministry provided additional machinery and the majority of firms made up entire instruments, though Hilger, Aldis, and Taylor, Taylor &

*Men working in Cookes' factory, World War I.*

Hobson served as optical workers to the trade. Behind this flag-waving endeavour, the government's purchase of German optical instruments through the back door of a neutral Switzerland suggests a certain lack of confidence.

Meanwhile, Dennis Taylor retired in July 1915 and was succeeded by G. S. E. Caillard. Thomas Cooke junior retired in October the same year, and Vickers put Francis Henry Barker on the Board, which from November 1915 met at Vickers House, Broadway, Westminster.

In 1916 the Directors decided to take a controlling interest in Adam Hilger Ltd. This company, established around 1875 by the German immigrants Adam and Otto

Hilger, enjoyed a high reputation for optical instruments based on prisms – spectroscopes and rangefinders in particular. Frank Twyman (1876-1959), their Managing Director, was professionally Dennis Taylor's equal as an optical designer. During the war, half the capacity was taken up by contract work for Barr & Stroud of Glasgow, manufacturers of large naval rangefinders. Hilgers also built the small Marindin rangefinder. They were actively trying to interest industrial chemists in new spectroscopes, but feared that trade would decline after the war. Consequently, Twyman and his Directors were not averse to a link with Cooke, and in 1916 Cooke's purchased 6,000 shares, giving them a six-tenths holding in Adam Hilger Ltd. According to Twyman, it was only when negotiations reached their final stages that he became aware that most of the shares in Cooke's were in fact held by Vickers.

Something of a renaissance had set in about 1912 with regard to the design and manufacture of surveying instruments, and the revolution imposed by wartime conditions was turned to good account in subsequent years. A bright future seemed assured for Jeffcott's tacheometer, patented by him in 1919 and manufactured by Cooke's. This was one of many instruments now offered to mining and construction engineers for fast accurate profiling. Cooke's standard tacheometer was offered in the shape of a 'South African Model' from 1920. Like the various 'Rand' models, its vertical circle was enclosed in a guard, it could sight down through an open-head tripod, and it came with a spare diaphragm, all features intended to appeal to mining engineers.

Dennis Taylor's younger son had joined Cooke's in 1908. Edward Wilfred Taylor (1891-1980) had been educated at Oundle, and had hoped to follow his brother to university. His father decided otherwise, and thus it was that Wilfred took up an apprenticeship, combining practical work with evening study. In 1912 he was sent to the United States as Cooke's sole representative, to attend a series of trials of coastal fire-control equipment. These trials were subsequently repeated in Britain, and led to orders being received from the governments of Spain and Russia and, during the First World War, from the British Admiralty. In 1914 he spent a period in the works of Taylor, Taylor & Hobson at Leicester. At some stage – it is not clear when – he worked at Hilgers, learning about interferometry which, as Twyman relates, stood him in good stead in later years.

Soon after the outbreak of war, Taylor enlisted in the army and found himself instructing officers in the use of rangefinders. He was wounded in France, and after having recovered was transferred to Scapa Flow, where he was engaged in checking battleship fire-control apparatus. From this remote outpost, he returned for the final years of the war to occupy a desk in Whitehall,

*Bishophill No. 2 Shop: 'Mr Jones' Fitting Shop', c1920.*

taking responsibility for re-equipping the whole fleet with searchlights. This complicated programme for the design, manufacture and delivery of equipment, occupied him until demobilization in 1919.

Wilfred Taylor returned to a Cooke's now under Vickers' control. In 1920 they learnt that William and James Simms were looking for a buyer for Troughton & Simms, one of Cookes' main competitors in the field of astronomical and surveying instruments. Vickers sanctioned Cooke's purchase of 16,500 £1 shares in the company, giving them a controlling interest, persuaded by the fact that Troughton & Simms operated more economically than Cooke's, producing competitive goods at lower prices. Cooke's had superior plant and better methods, but lacked effective management. Business declined notwithstanding. Vickers were obliged to support Cooke's, holding the shares in Hilger and in Troughton & Simms as security. In 1921 these shares were transferred to Vickers outright, to cancel Cooke's loan of £39,000 and to guarantee their overdraft of £45,000. By 1922 work was urgently needed; indeed the situation was so desperate that the Directors were persuaded to forego their fees. In the hope that joint trading would improve matters, the two boards agreed to amalgamate their respective companies. Capital was increased to £105,000, by the issue of 20,000 new shares and Troughton & Simms went into voluntary liquidation, allowing Cooke's to purchase the buildings, stock, plant and goodwill for £21,000.

In 1922 the combined business reformed as Cooke, Troughton & Simms, with its Head Office at York. Production, including Troughton & Simms' current contracts, was transferred to York. Part of Charlton Works was retained for repair work and the rest disposed of to Johnson & Phillips, engineers. James Simms' nephew James Simms Wilson moved north as a Director of the new company, whilst his son Arthur

*Surveyors on the Shackleton-Rowett Antarctic Expedition, 1921.*

Simms remained in London as Sales Manager, where, the Fleet Street lease having expired in 1921, he operated from 3-5 Broadway, Westminster, in the shadow of Vickers House.

*Watkin depression rangefinder, for gun crews ranging out to sea from cliff-top forts. Early 20th century.*

# Part Three – Cooke, Troughton & Simms

## Chapter 9: Under Vickers' Control

COOKE, TROUGHTON & SIMMS did their collective best to beef up trade in a dull market. Customers were circulated with offers of increased discounts on large purchases: up to 25% on certain telescopes, decreasing to 15% for standard theodolites and levels, 5% for tacheometers. In 1923 Vickers set up British Separators as a subsidiary to Centrifugal Separators, a company in which they had a small investment, delegating the manufacture of its machinery to Cooke's, who badly needed work. They were also encouraged to exhibit on Vickers' stand at the British Empire Exhibition of 1924-25 where they displayed their range of optical and surveying instruments, plus industrial instruments originating with Vickers, of which more later. This reorganisation failed to cure the underlying malaise, caused by an inflated product range being stocked on a declining market. By 1926 both Centrifugal and British Separators were in financial difficulties and Cooke's ended up being paid with shares, though they continued to manufacture until 1936 when the business was sold to the Alfa-Laval Co. Ltd. Annual losses mounted from £4,383 to £7,967 and then £16,183, and in addition £22,516 was owed as Excess Profits Duty and Munitions Levy in respect of wartime contracts. Eventually Vickers grew tired of pumping cash into an ailing company. Cooke's was allowed to go into voluntary liquidation, on the understanding that Vickers would appoint a committee to see if it could be reconstructed and made profitable.

At the time of liquidation, Cookes' York premises consisted of three factories, with a drawing office,

*Cooke, Troughton & Simms' offices, 3 Broadway, Westminster, 1920-30.*

leather and paint shops, plus Bishophill House and other houses in the surrounding streets. Charlton Works occupied about one acre, with approximately 25,000 square feet of covered space. There were London offices at Broadway and the shop and workshop at Cape Town. Other assets included plant, property such as the valuable list of patents, goodwill, debts and contracts. In July 1924 the company was advertised for sale in the national and trade press, attracting enquiries but no offers. In the autumn of 1924 Vickers bought it for the sum of £75,000. At this stage, the pneumatic despatch tubes business, which Frederick Cooke had set up some 40 years previously, was sold off to the Sturtevant Engineering Co. Ltd for £1,500. Robert Wigglesworth, who had been with the company for 45 years, retired, remaining on the Board of Adam Hilger. The company was re-established as Cooke, Troughton & Simms Ltd with Sir Trevor Dawson (1866-1931) as Chairman and other Vickers nominees on the Board. Despite this change of ownership, the employees, and indeed the other citizens of York, continued to refer to the factory as 'Cookes', a practice which we shall follow here.

Adam Hilger Ltd was left to its own devices until about 1926 when Vickers sought to bring it into line with their other associated companies. This would have entailed making a contribution towards the expenses of the central office which in Twyman's opinion, would not benefit Hilger's. He refused to carry out Vickers' instructions and, after what he described as 'amicable discussions' and several attempts to find another purchaser, Twyman himself bought the shares by instalments, concluding the deal in 1930.

*The perils of surveying – probably Cape Point, South Africa, c1923.*

In the postwar years European makers were marketing new types of theodolite that were far in advance of British designs. The man largely responsible was a Swiss surveyor, Heinrich Wild, who worked with Zeiss before establishing his own business at Heerbrugg in Switzerland in 1921. Wild's aim was to build a lightweight theodolite, where the observer would not have to leave the telescope in order to take his two readings on the circle, but would have both presented to him at a single eyepiece, aligned by a single-screw micrometer. This entailed a radical redesign of the theodolite body, to contain the complex optical system. Wild's specification was ready in 1919 and by 1921 his theodolites were coming off the production lines at the Zeiss works. These theodolites were indeed small and handy. Their circles were divided on glass. Readings from opposite sides of the circle were brought through an internal optical system and presented together against a fiducial line, at the eyepiece. This enabled the instruments to be sealed and thus impervious to rain, dust and the shocks of transport. Whilst they fell short of the accuracy demanded for primary triangulation, Canadian experience showed that the 3¾-inch theodolites matched up to a good British 12-inch.

The military implications of such findings boded ill for the British export market. To decide what action to take, a conference was convened in 1926 at Tavistock, in Devonshire, attended by officers from the Admiralty, the War Office and the Ordnance Survey, along with representatives from Cooke, Troughton & Simms (who sent E. W. Taylor, A. D. Simms and John Linn), E. R. Watts & Son, and C. F. Casella & Co. The conference members went onto Dartmoor to test continental theodolites against the latest British models. Afterwards, suitably chastened, the instrument makers returned home with instructions to try to divise a similar theodolite which did not infringe existing patents. Casella's took no further action and E. R. Watts came to an agreement with Zeiss and incorporated several German patents in their design. Cooke, Troughton & Simms found their way round the foreign patents and came up with the first British double-reading optical micrometer theodolite, appropriately named the 'Tavistock'.

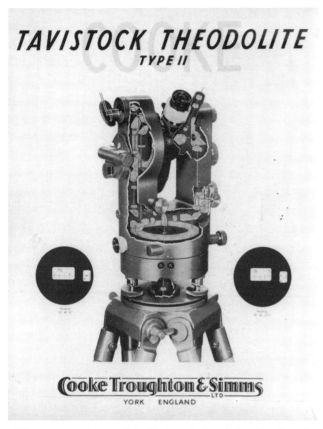

*Military surveyors with a Tavistock theodolite.*

*Diagrammatic view of the Tavistock theodolite showing the interior optical parts.*

The Tavistock patents were filed in the names of Captain T. Y. Baker RN and R. W. Cheshire of the National Physical Laboratory, who until recently had been Assistant Optical Manager at Cooke's. The first field tests showed up defects in the illumination system, but Wilfred Taylor was able to correct this. The slow process of dividing and etching each circle individually was soon replaced by a fast photographic technique, more appropriate to mass production. A 3½-inch Tavistock, reading to one second of arc, weighed

11½ lbs, and as packed with its accessories in a duralumin case with outer canvas cover, 22½ lbs; it was hoped to further reduce the weight of production models.

The Tavistock went into production from 1930. The first example to reach South Africa was put on display in the Johannesburg agency that year and it became available for purchase early in 1931. Its telescope could transit completely and thus take zenith readings – which gave it the edge over its continental rivals – but local reports indicated that it was inferior in other respects. After a flurry of correspondence between Baker and the

South African surveyors, who were after all less familiar with it than Baker and Wilfred Taylor, the results obtained at York were accepted and the Tavistock was widely employed. It had arrived at exactly the right time, when several primary surveys were in hand. The geodetic Tavistock, which followed it off the production line soon afterwards, read to half a second of arc. The surveyors generally carried more than one make of theodolite, probably because none of them performed perfectly in all situations.

In 1926 Cooke's publicised their 'Universal milling and shaping machine', product of some 60 years' of development. Over the years, various fitments had been added to a basic machine which made it in effect a universal jig, capable of rapidly turning out standard parts. Some 20 of these machines were being run at Buckingham Works, and presumably Cooke's were happy to make and sell them to the trade. The firm, as might be expected, prided themselves on the accuracy of their divided circles. Cooke's had built themselves another engine in 1907, and in 1919 they bought a fourth from the Société Genevoise. By 1933 one of their eight-inch theodolites that had been employed on the Gold Coast Survey was reported as having a maximum error of $\frac{1}{60,000}$. In surveying terms this represented an error of less than one foot at a distance of 40 miles – 'surely a triumph of mind and machine . . . the actual placing of a readable mark on the limb of an instrument to [this] accuracy would seem to transcend the *mechanical* limit of human endeavour'.

———

The Optical Convention of 1926 was the setting for Cooke's to exhibit industrial machines manufactured primarily for Vickers and their associated companies. Among these was the 'Heape-Grylls cinema machine' for ballistics experiments; seeing, for example, what happened when shells struck armour plate. The idea had come from W. Heape FRS and H. B. Grylls, and it was designed by Professor C. V. Boys and developed by Cooke, Troughton & Simms to the order of the British government. Its ingenious system of lenses and mirrors

*Cookes' advertisement for repairs, 1927.*

shot 500 to 5,000 frames per second, with exposures as brief as $\frac{1}{65,000}$ of a second. A substantial and sturdy monster, with its film drum, lens wheels, drive shafts etc, it weighed in at four tons. Another military exhibit was the hand-held Waymouth-Cooke rangefinder, which gave the observer the range of any ship whose mast-height or length was known to him. The Fereday-Palmer Stress Recorder had military and civil engineering applications, being designed to measure rapidly-fluctuating stresses such as might be experienced on railway bridges or ships' hulls. Basically an industrial seismograph, its horizontal pendulum responded to small vibrations, and by reflecting a beam of light, magnified and recorded these movements onto a moving strip of photographic paper. The Vickers Hardness Testing Machine impressed a diamond against the test piece and registered its hardness on the standard Brinell scale.

Notwithstanding these new products, Cooke, Troughton & Simms were as deep in the slump as other optical instrument manufacturers. Wartime experience had shown that certain key industries were largely in foreign hands and the Safeguarding of Industries Act, 1921, had been intended to stimulate domestic growth in those industries by imposing a duty of 33⅓% *ad valorem* on all goods imported from outside the British Empire. The optical glass, and optical and electrical instruments industries were seen to be candidates for this protection. Nevertheless, when a Board of Trade Committee reported in 1926 on the effects of this Act, it found that accumulated stocks of optical glass and instruments, the subsequent fall-off in military orders, and the imports from countries with cheaper labour costs and favourable exchange rates, combined to reduce domestic orders, whilst foreign tariffs reduced the opportunity for export. The Act was not watertight, for it failed to stop foreign imported parts being 'made-up' in Commonwealth countries and then imported free of duty. Nor did the government's own practice of selling off war surplus help matters. Of the 20 optical instrument makers who survived the war, three had since gone into liquidation.

Cookes' salesman W. H. Connell went round Spain in 1927, and to South America and Canada the following year, reinforcing links with agents and trying to persuade them to deal only in Cooke, Troughton & Simms instruments. He talked to groups of engineers and surveyors, published articles in the local trade press, and took note of local conventions, such as the undervaluing of instruments so as to reduce customs duties, and the preference for instruments to carry the name of the agent, rather than the manufacturer. It was deemed advisable, however, to register Cookes' name in Argentina to prevent its use by unscrupulous dealers and this registration was renewed until 1971. In Spain Connell found a legacy of 'Troughton' goodwill, but in America the firm was known simply as 'Cooke'. Everywhere it faced serious competition from Zeiss and Wild; in Canada there was some competition from the United States firm of Keuffel & Esser. It was acknowledged that Cooke, Troughton & Simms instruments were superior, but they were generally more expensive and in the hands of semi-skilled surveyors this quality was money wasted. Connell returned from the Americas convinced of the 'tremendous sales possibilities'. As he

*Vickers Projection Microscope Mk III, 1941.*

told his potential customers, the modern demand for quickly-read, light and compact surveying instruments had resulted in some startling departures from conventional designs. Circles of three inches diameter could be read direct to one second of arc. Generally speaking, transits and levels now weighed and bulked one-third less than their pre-war equivalents. The catalogue of surveying instruments had been pruned down. Of the old pattern of levels, only the Cooke reversible remained, now accompanied by the new 'self-checking' level, a co-operative venture between Cooke and E. R. Watts. And he declared to his Canadian readers, 'A

*Cookes' stand at the Buenos Aires Exhibition, 1931, shared with nautical instruments by Heath & Co.*

prosperous and efficient instrument industry is essential to the nation's welfare, especially as war becomes more and more a matter of long-range destruction, and in this connection the British instrument makers owe a debt of gratitude to the engineers and surveyors of our far-flung Empire whose patronage is helping them to pull through these lean post-war years.'

Connell's exhortations fell on deaf ears. Wilfred Taylor remembered 1929 as the year that 'the demand for optical instruments ceased almost overnight'. For three years, first-class men were laid off and the shops almost closed down. Cooke, Troughton & Simms took a stand at the British Industries Fair, held at Buenos Aires in 1931, where they showed off the Jeffcott and Tavistock instruments. In 1932 only the Optics Department was busy, mainly with ordnance work for Vickers-Armstrongs. The York main factory was running at 40% of capacity. Again Vickers came to the rescue, this time with the Vickers Projection Microscope. This was a toolroom microscope which accepted specimens of metal weighing up to 50 lbs and projecting an image which could be photographed or viewed directly. It had

been developed by R. L. Smith at Vickers' Research Establishment some 10 years previously. Its manufacture was assigned to Charlton Works in 1932 and this, with maintenance work for government, railways and colliery contracts, kept the southern factory turning over at 50% of capacity. The number of workmen was being reduced to offset the net financial loss. With a general recession in industry and in civil engineering construction, prospects for surveying and industrial instruments were bleak. Nevertheless, the managers put in hand a thorough reorganisation of their manufacturing structure, though at the years' end Simms Wilson reported to Vickers 'the prospects are considered to be the worst on record'.

From time to time the gloom lifted – sundry manufacturing contracts were picked up to keep the machinery turning. Even bottle-making machinery and toy microscopes kept the men occupied. By June 1933 the York factory was only 30% employed and net losses had risen. The situation being generally bad throughout the trade, tenders were extremely competitive, and Cooke's seldom won a contract. However, the restructuring was beginning to pay off; a batch of theodolites came off the new production line at two-thirds the previous cost. The Vickers Projection Microscope (now built at York) were selling well and by the autumn a new and cheaper version – priced at £90 as against £230 – came into production. Old Thomas Cooke had sold optical microscopes in the early years of his business, Cooke's had re-entered the field by way of industrial metrology and were now competent to secure an important order for medical microscopes. A new engineers' level, listed at £16 to £18 as against former prices of around £27, and a new precise level, offered the chance of competing successfully against Zeiss. The microscope range was broadened, with instruments aimed at the medical, industrial and educational markets. In an effort to cut costs still further, work was transferred from skilled to unskilled men and apprentices – even to women.

In 1932 the British Association held its Annual Meeting at York. Touring the district, as was the custom, the members (who included H. D. Taylor) saw Cooke's last astronomical transit in the early stages of construction at Buckingham Works. This was a reversible transit circle, with a telescope of seven inches aperture and focal length of eight feet, designed by Wilfred Taylor. Its 28-inch circles, divided on glass, were the largest of their kind that had been made. When it was finished and under test at York, its weight-relieving apparatus was found to be unsatisfactory and had to be redesigned. A year passed before it could be delivered to Greenwich. There it was found that the pivots of the transit axis were not truly circular and they had to be reground on site. Harold Spencer Jones, Astronomer Royal, lent them a Krupp Mikrotast gauge for this purpose and remarked later to Grubbs that if Cooke's had owned such a tool, they would have saved themselves much time and effort. Indeed it seems strange that a firm which prided itself on

its engineering metrology should lack such equipment. Other serious defects were then revealed, and the transit was returned to York in April 1937. By the time it was set up, Cooke's had decided that such large individual instruments were no longer profitable. In the summer of 1938 they sold the astronomical side of the business to their hitherto competitors, Grubb, Parsons Ltd, of Newcastle. A subsequent schedule of costs and 'what went wrong?' shows astonishingly that Cooke's had been expected to estimate on sketches from the book *History and description of the Royal Observatory, Cape of Good Hope* plus some photos of the collimators. They seriously overran their contract price of £4,750 and were afterwards granted a further £1,500. When he checked the circle graduations, Spencer Jones was intrigued by the fluctuating and periodic errors and in 1941-42 he corresponded with Wilfred Taylor on the method of dividing that had been used. Taylor explained that the divisions had been cut not by engine but by a special method of generation devised by Cooke's. Spencer Jones was not impressed.

The 'East African Arc' was surveyed with one of the first geodetic Tavistocks and a special eight-inch reflecting theodolite equipped with micrometer and sensitive levels, made by Cooke's. A Wild geodetic theodolite was also taken. The baseline for the arc was measured with a new apparatus known as the Macca Base Measurement Gear which had been designed by G. T. McCaw in conjunction with Cooke, Troughton & Simms, consisting of 100-feet invar tapes made by Chesterman which were strained over pulleys to a fixed weight and graduated where they passed under the measuring head. It was said of this gear that 'it must be the only first model of a surveying instrument which has not occasioned widespread controversy and complaint: this presumably because of its design by co-operation between surveyor and instrument maker'.

The Macca gear was also used to measure bases in the re-triangulation of Great Britain which commenced in 1935. The angles were taken with 5-inch and 5½-inch Tavistocks, working at night with electric beam lamps

*E. Wilfred Taylor (1891-1980).*

also manufactured by Cooke's. Zeiss levels were employed on the English stages, being replaced by Cooke levels when the surveyors reached Scotland.

Gradually trade improved, helped by an upturn in overseas civil orders, and as the contracts taken on at rock-bottom prices worked their way through the system. In 1934 a huge ordnance order brought Cooke, Troughton & Simms back to 100% capacity and as similar orders went to other manufacturers, there was a general shortage of trained instrument makers. Cooke's found themselves with one-third of their workforce composed of apprentices under the age of 18, a proportion that increased to nearly two-thirds by 1935.

At the British Industries Fair held at Birmingham in 1935 Cooke's exhibited three toolroom appliances designed to serve the now recovering metallurgical industry. The Vickers Projection Microscope and the Vickers Contour Projection Apparatus were both devices which threw enlarged images of specimens onto a screen and, in the case of the Contour Projection Apparatus, measured for accuracy of manufacture. Cooke's own Optical Comparator was also for examining manufactured parts.

---

In 1936 Sir Thomas Inskip, Attorney-General and later minister for co-ordination of defence, called the optical instrument makers together and gave them a list of military requirements. Cooke, Troughton & Simms secured a contract whereby the government would re-equip Cooke's No. 2 factory and bring it back into production the following year. Such was the upturn in business, that the managers became worried that orders might exceed capacity. In fact throughout the 1930s they had become increasingly handicapped by old and unsatisfactory buildings. The total floor area was 70,000 square feet, but it was dispersed over four separate sites and the workshops were small and at different levels, so that machinery could not be easily transferred from one site to another. The result was a continual expenditure to adapt the buildings to meet every new situation as it arose and clearly it was time to move out and start afresh

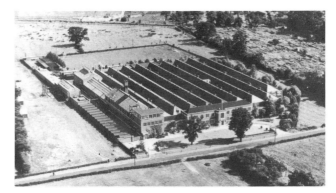

*Haxby Road Works, York, an aerial view.*

elsewhere. In 1937 the managers therefore began to look for a site which met certain conditions of size, access to roads and mains services, and suchlike. It is interesting to note that the principal factor was their wish to stay within two, or at most three, miles of York city centre, so as to retain their skilled workforce, now standing at 700 men.

After investigating a number of possibilities, Cooke's were able to purchase a site on Haxby Road which had emerged as their first choice. It was 1.65 miles from York Railway Station, 5.5 acres in extent, with all mains services, and the buildings could be laid out to receive north light. The factory was built during 1939. It was a one-storey building, designed to accommodate 1,000 workers. There was no need to install shafting to drive the machinery, since for some years only motorised machines had been purchased and the old shaft-driven machines were now discarded. The main manufacturing area of nearly 81,000 square feet would be free of walls, any internal divisions consisting of lightweight moveable partitions. It would be separated from the wing of 11,800 square feet housing the repair departments and the foundry and joinery, which created fumes and dust, and presented a higher fire risk.

At the outbreak of war, the Ministry of Supply and the War Office called for a large quantity of sighting telescopes and theodolites, besides commandeering much of the civil output of surveying instruments. The number of employees rose to 900, but there was a desperate need for skilled men and Cooke's warned that deliveries would be held back if the government continued to call up apprentices. By 1940, the supply of raw materials was the determining factor on output. The new factory, which was named 'Kingsway North' in the hope of disguising its true whereabouts from enemy spies, was in full production by the year's end. Negotiations had been opened with Messrs Rowntree to take over part of their premises – known as Hambleton – where another 300 employees would make military telescopes and Vickers tank periscopes. There was some delay before the promised American machine tools arrived, but by the autumn of 1941 production was under way and in 1943 optical work formerly carried out at Bishophill was also transferred there. The new range of optical measuring tools were in great demand throughout the engineering industry, Cooke's being only one of several firms specialising in such apparatus. Cookes' experience at dividing on glass had led to the development of their Optical Dividing Head, where a glass master was optically compared to copy-divide other circles and to measure angular divisions. Basically the same as the Zeiss Dividing Head, it was capable of generating circles of little more than an inch radius, with errors kept under one second of arc. Cooke's Toolroom Microscope was likewise a close copy of the Zeiss model. The medical profession took Cooke, Troughton & Simms microscopes in place of those formerly obtained from Germany. By 1941, factory output was four times that of the pre-war period; the workforce was nearing 2,000 people, nearly one-quarter of them women, and the value of orders on hand exceeded £1,000,000. The Johannesburg workshop was similarly engaged on military contracts from the South African Government.

By late 1942 Kingsway North (now camouflaged) had been extended to increase the output of gunsight telescopes. Women constituted 40% of the workforce of 2,500. Cooke's were asked to supply theodolites and other instruments to the US forces, similar instruments not being available in the USA. Three hundred Vickers Projection Microscopes had been delivered and 60 more were on order, chiefly for the aircraft industry. Apart from a one-day strike by employees dissatisfied with the Arbitration Awards, harmony appears to have reigned.

1943 marked the peak of production. Orders for optical munitions then eased, though Cooke's carried on at full strength for longer than other optical firms as they were supplying equipment for the desert campaign. Cookes' managers were determined not to be caught unprepared for peace as they had been after World War One. Some of their planned products were already part of the wartime output, and this had allowed them to tool up and in some cases begin manufacture. They proposed firstly, a new range of theodolites and levels; secondly, industrial instruments for which Zeiss had previously held the market; and thirdly, biological and metallurgical microscopes. Wilfred Taylor, whilst in the USA to discuss naval rangefinders, had been to look over the factories of Kodak, Bausch & Lomb, Keuffel & Esser, the Spencer Lens Co., and Polaroid. He reported that 'the American optical industry was in a very virile condition' and spending far more on research and development than its British counterparts.

Towards the end of hostilities, civil orders began to dominate the order book. Export licences were obtained to allow Cooke's to restock the South African branches, starved of products by the shortage of shipping capacity and having to survive on locally-made products. The Ministry of Supply came forward with orders for microscopes. On the debit side, the unskilled workforce was incapable of meeting the exacting standards called for in the new range of civil instruments. Clearly, recruitment and training would have to figure large in the postwar programme if Cooke's were to regain their former status in the optical industry.

This is perhaps the place to comment on Cookes' attitude to training, for it is an aspect of the firm's history that merits further investigation. The firm maintained the good reputation that it had acquired during the days of Thomas Cooke senior, its former apprentices and craftsmen being respected and indeed sought after by

*Cookes' M4000 microscope, 1944.*

catered to the Clerkenwell optical tradesmen in the late 19th century, and was one of the few institutions which continued to teach technical optics into the 20th century. Between about 1955 and 1975 Cooke, Troughton & Simms was one of several optical firms contributing to a bursary at Imperial College, London.

*Cookes' employees with 25 years' service, photographed in March, 1912. Front row, left to right: A. Taylor, C. Rotherham, S. Yardley, J. Douglas, G. Wilson, T. Patterson, M. Muller, H. D. Taylor. 2nd row: B. Smithson, F. Ashworth, W. Gill, W. Johnson, W. Harrison, J. Graham, T. Pashley, H. Peats, T. Nelson. 3rd row: W. Eyeington, A. Harrison, W. Smallwood, J. Colley, J. Metcalfe, G. Milner, T. Jefferson, G. Dinsdale. Back row: J. Illingworth, A. Sutherland, E. Ridsdill, A. Pashley, W. H. Jones, T. Dwyer, H. Shepherd, J. Jackson, A. Waddingham. (Mr A. A. Harrison, who retired in 1946 after 64 years service, always objected to being photographed and so does not appear here.)*

other engineering establishments in the district – notably the railway and ordnance workshops. The number of photographs showing groups of employees with more than 25 years' service suggests, however, that by and large, Cookes' men stayed loyal to their employer.

School-leavers who became apprentices attended classes at York Technical School, and links were forged, through Wilfred Taylor's involvement with the Technical Optics Committee, with Finsbury Technical College (later the Northampton Institute and now City University), and with Imperial College, London. Finsbury had

# Chapter 10: Short Focus, Wide Field

COOKES' FACTORIES WERE NOT IN FULL production in September 1945 when civil orders for microscopes were beginning to come in. Before reorganising the factory for this work, and vacating Rowntree's premises, Wilfred Taylor joined a Ministry of Supply party which visited the Zeiss and Leitz optical works in Germany, where he was able to make a thorough investigation of layout and processes. He subsequently reported that a specialised machine 'captured' from Zeiss was proving very useful in connection with microscope manufacture.

Post-war prospects looked good. So much equipment had been destroyed in Europe and demand was rising in the Far East. Medical science had progressed but the laboratories had been unable to buy modern instruments. Cooke's began to set up agencies in Europe, accepted trainee mechanics from their Indian and Australian agencies and dedicated part of the factory to the training of apprentices. Looking over their collective shoulder, the managers decided that United States competition was nothing to worry about, but they were unhappy about the 'potential menace' of Swiss instruments. Cooke's designed a range of medical microscopes that could view by incident, transmitted and polarised light, and take photographs, and built to specifications and prices from 'student' to advanced 'research' levels. They improved microscope lighting so as to give even-field illumination. They had their own version of the phase-contrast microscope, for biologists examining living tissue. Their petrological microscopes were the first to have been made in quantity in Britain – Leitz having held the pre-war market. They offered a range of metallurgical microscopes and were adapting this instrument into a micro-hardness testing apparatus. They were working on the development of an ultra-violet microscope but experiencing difficulties with its fine-motion mechanism. The Vickers Projection Microscope was selling at two per week. This agreeable situation ended when the bitterly cold winter of 1946-47 brought a fuel crisis which slowed down all industrial production, delaying the already extended delivery times of raw materials and components.

The South African branches recovered well enough and by 1947 were selling more Cookes' products than factored items. Cooke's exhibited at numerous trade and private shows, and played host to visiting groups from the Institution of Mechanical Engineers and the Commonwealth Survey Officers Conference. Those Conference members who had not previously visited Cookes' works were impressed by its size. Many had also assumed that scientific instruments were still individually made. It was explained that though bubble-making, assembly and optical testing were still craft processes, most of the work was highly mechanised. They were shown a display of the jigs and tools required for one particular theodolite, and the range of Cooke, Troughton & Simms surveying instruments plus a prototype tacheometer derived from a Zeiss pattern.

At the end of 1947 the long-standing problem over the use of the name Cooke as trademark for the 'Cooke' lens was at last resolved. This concerned Dennis Taylor's triplet which had been licensed to Taylor, Taylor & Hobson from about 1883 until its patent expired. In fact

Taylors had continued to advertise as 'Cooke lenses' other photographic and ciné lenses unrelated to Dennis Taylor's patent. Fortunately the two firms' directors were on friendly terms, but even so their respective lawyers and patent agents were called in to advise. Cooke, Troughton & Simms wished to retain their right to advertise their products informally as 'Cookes', to avoid using their cumbersome full name. United Kingdom laws did not normally permit a simple surname to be registered as a trademark, but this was allowed in certain foreign countries. Accordingly it was agreed that Taylors could register 'Cooke' lenses in Argentina and Brazil, while Cooke's could use that name to market their own products in those countries.

———

Within the city boundary, Thomas Cooke's original Buckingham Works – No. 1 Factory – empty since 1939, was sold in 1948 to the Northeastern Electricity Board. No. 2 Factory, built in 1916, still accepted contract work on its government-owned machinery. Skilled labour was becoming scarce but productivity was steadily raised by better organisation. In January 1949 a two-week exhibition was staged in the factory, to show employees how Cooke, Troughton & Simms products were serving science and industry. School-children were also invited to the exhibition, in the hope of attracting some of them into apprenticeships.

Danger signs had appeared by the end of 1947 when Swiss instruments and German microscopes were marketed at 30% to 40% below British prices, and this situation continued to worry the directors. In Canada, however, new branches were opened in Toronto in 1950, and later in Montreal and Edmonton, and a branch in Salisbury, Southern Rhodesia, opened in 1958. The old-established branches in Cape Town and Johannesburg were registered locally in 1957 as Cooke, Troughton & Simms South Africa (Pty) Ltd. An American off-shoot was created in 1958 by acquiring the assets of R. Y. Ferner, former agents in Boston, now registered as Cooke, Troughton & Simms Inc. At home, Cooke's, so dependant on exports, was periodically frustrated by one or other of its agents failing to secure import

*Lens polishing at Haxby Road, early 1950s.*

licences. This left the factory with stock which, if it was non-standard, might not find another buyer.

The post-war recovery boom was soon braked by the deteriorating international situation. When NATO was set up in 1949 Cooke's were once more called on to supply optical munitions and at that stage virtually abandoned their interest in non-optical industrial tools. However, armaments contracts had to be fought for by cutting prices and offering prompt delivery. This often meant overtime or night-shift working, which ate into the profit. After finishing the contract, men might have to be put on short time until sufficient civil work could be drummed up. But civil exports also had to be priced competitively, and at one stage Cooke's absorbed the costs of a wages increase by loading the home prices so as to keep export prices steady, a practice they later recognised as unwise.

In December 1951 the managers reported that the profits had reached a record peacetime high – and so had the tax bill. On the down side, they noted that Japanese survey instruments were now penetrating the Canadian market.

The Drawing Office Materials Department that had been set up as a Vickers Group service in the old

*Arthur Simms (1891-1976).*

*James Simms Wilson (1893-1976).*

Charlton Works moved after the war to Chelsea, and in 1952, to Euston. It enjoyed a healthy turnover but apart from sharing the name of Cooke, Troughton & Simms and their old 'Castle' brand name, it had little to do with the York business. Twenty years later it moved to Coulsdon and in 1978 Vickers disposed of it.

In 1956 it was decided to upgrade the Vickers Projection Microscope and the new version was selling well by 1962. However a Mark IV proved extremely troublesome to design and as the 18-month manufacturing cycle posed a high investment risk for each batch and tied up more money than the company could afford, its manufacture ceased in 1972 after 50 years of useful life.

James Simms Wilson and Arthur Simms both retired in 1956, ending a family tie with the firm that had begun

in the 1820s. Wilfred Taylor retired the same year, keeping his seat on the Board as a non-executive Director until 1961. Many honours had been bestowed on Taylor over the years: a CBE after World War Two, election to the Royal Society in 1952, Honorary Doctorates from Leeds in 1957 and from York in 1977 – consolation, one must hope, for the disappointment that he had felt on being obliged to go straight from school to factory bench – and other professional honours. These were his reward for long service on training and advisory committees and various national technical bodies. Outside the hours of business, Taylor took a lively interest in all aspects of Yorkshire wildlife, and was an enthusiastic supporter of local organisations. To the workforce, many of whom had been at Cooke's for their

*Surveying with the Tellurometer, c1960.*

entire working life, the departure of Taylor and Simms Wilson must have seemed like the end of an era.

South Africa continued to be a fertile field for inventive surveyors. The Tellurometer – an instrument for measuring distance by means of radio-waves – was invented and first demonstrated there by T. L. Wadley. In 1956 P. D. Scott Maxwell, Cooke's next Managing Director, was tipped off by a friend who had seen this prototype demonstrated. Scott Maxwell went to South Africa and negotiated with the Tellurometer Propriety for distribution rights. Cooke, Troughton & Simms (S. Africa) became shareholders in the firm and as Tellurometer (UK) Ltd, operating from 1 January 1957, Cooke's acquired exclusive rights to sell the Tellurometer in Europe and its dependencies, and in the Indian sub-continent. Scott Maxwell pushed the Tellurometer sales and development, scoring some success with NATO and other military and civilian purchasers. Elsewhere, he reported, the outlook 'could be better'. In June 1958 he returned somewhat shaken from a visit to the United States, having realised the extent to which the British optical industry was handicapping itself by its high labour costs. Despite these alarm signals, no move was made at this time to re-equip with the latest machine tools.

———

In the 1950s the story becomes complicated by a new business practice of taking over manufacture of instruments designed elsewhere (and sometimes made simultaneously by other companies), and by the takeover of companies or parts of companies, in order to acquire some desirable patent or product. In this respect, Vickers allowed Cooke's a high degree of independence as long as they met their profit target. Wilfred Taylor, while responsible for the development of microscope and other objectives, was assisted by consultants such as the petrologist A. F. Hallimond, by J. Dyson of AEI, and by members of university and government scientific laboratories. In the 1950s Dyson and Tiller of the AEI Research Laboratory had designed an instrument for checking alignment on machine tools by means of a circular diffraction grating. This was manufactured under licence by Cooke's, further developed by Wilfred Taylor, and marketed under the name 'Rodolite'. The range of microscopes offered was broadened in 1959 by the acquisition of McArthur Microscopes Ltd, and the

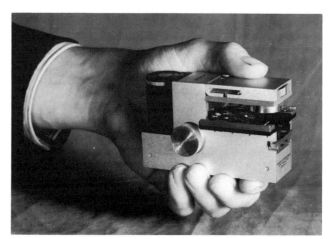

*Cooke-McArthur microscope, c1960.*

robust miniature field instrument derived from John McArthur's design of 1934. But the Cooke-McArthur microscope failed to live up to expectations and after a few years the companies went their separate ways.

The acquisition of C. Baker Ltd in 1959 brought immediate benefits. The original Charles Baker had founded his business in the late 18th century and it had since prospered on the sales of a wide range of good-quality microscopes and a thriving trade in second-hand instruments (including numerous reconditioned Cooke telescopes). Baker's Holborn shop and the sales and repair business stayed in the hands of Michael Curties, one of the Directors, who renamed it Rekab Ltd. Cooke's gained control of Baker's Croydon factory and, of greater value to them, the services of Francis Smith, internationally respected as an optical designer.

Around 1950 Smith – allegedly working in the summerhouse of his garden in Scarborough – had developed the interference microscope independently of its German progenitors. He built a mock-up in Cookes' research laboratories but no British manufacturer showed interest until Bakers hired him as an 'optical computer' (ie, designer) and he was able to convince them of its possibilities. It came onto the market in 1954 and was appreciated by biologists and the medical profession. Like the phase-contrast, to which it was the successor, the interference microscope showed up living tissue which could not be stained for normal examination.

In 1959 Cooke's also bought up Casella (Electronics) Ltd, offshoot formed in 1952 of a business dating back to the early years of the 19th century. At stake was Casella's series of blood and particle counters and the accompanying electronics. Product manufacture was moved to York and the development side went into a new extension to Baker's Croydon factory. This brought the total number of employees to around 1,100, of whom 800 were at York.

It was clearly impractical to add Baker's name to those of Cooke, Troughton and Simms on the actual products or on their advertisements. A new company,

*Francis Smith.*

Vickers Instruments Ltd, was registered in 1962 and acquired the assets of Cooke, Troughton & Simms Ltd, trading under that rubric from 1 January, 1963. At the same time, Cooke, Troughton & Simms (without the Ltd) was registered as the business name of the small ophthalmic business, run formerly from 17 Broadway, then from Stag Place, Victoria, until it was sold in June 1985. Subsequently, the Vickers Instruments Division was formed to hold Vickers Instruments and Vickers Instruments' other trade-related companies under a single management umbrella.

1959 saw the removal of the protection afforded by the Safeguarding of Industries Act of 1921 (mentioned in Chapter 9). The duty, then standing at 45%, was progressively reduced, obliging Cooke's to restructure its working methods once more in order to temper the chill wind of competition. The managers' joy at holding down production costs evaporated when they realised that lower profits made it impossible to cut home prices to meet the domestic competition that would follow if and when Britain joined the Common Market. And somehow they had to absorb the wage awards, shorter working week, and increased holiday allowance which Cookes' long-serving employees now enjoyed. It was, as the Vickers' Group Chairman reported, 'a difficult year'.

The York factory remained profitable; the Croydon Works, with its output of less sophisticated microscopes, did not. In 1968 all microscope stock and work in hand was moved to York. The Croydon workforce was directed to produce the Vickers Cytology Scanning Apparatus and the following year both factory and product were transferred to Vickers' Medical Division.

In connection with these transfers, a thoroughgoing programme of plant and machinery overhaul was put in hand in 1966. An air-conditioned space for processing optical parts had been created in 1958; now two new glass-polishing shops were fitted up and a battery of high-productivity machine tools installed.

Throughout the 1960s the Vickers Instruments Annual Reports present a competent and active business, developing surveying instruments, increasing the range of microscopes to satisfy all classes of user, securing ordnance contracts, and achieving record levels of orders, sales and profits. In fact the true state of affairs was considerably less rosy. By the 1970s profit margins had declined. Profits on surveying and ordnance

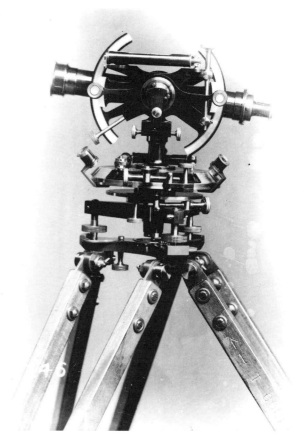

*Everest theodolite in its 20th century form.*

instruments failed to support, on the one hand, the extensive dealer network and on the other, the substantial development costs. In December 1973 a fuel crisis coupled to widespread industrial disputes forced the government to impose a three-day working week until March 1974, which took a further toll of profits.

Cooke's disposed of Tellurometer (UK) Ltd to Plessey around 1965. They did not follow European manufacturers of surveying instruments who by the late 1960s were making significant changes to theodolite design and taking advantage of solid-state electronics. Zeiss produced their electronic tacheometer in 1968, and by 1977 Wild, Kern and Hewlett-Packard were marketing their 'total stations' – systems embracing angle measurement, electronic distance measurement and a microprocessor within a single casing. Cooke's meanwhile concentrated on improved versions of the old conventional theodolites and levels although the domestic market for these instruments dried up each time the government imposed building restrictions. It seems that Cooke's paid a high price for their independence, since Vickers never viewed them as potential leaders in their field. Cooke's maintained a small research and development department, and had a loyal and experienced workforce, yet Vickers chose not to grant them the substantial funding that might have kept them abreast of their competitors.

Nevertheless, occasional bright stars shone through the gloom: in 1969 Cooke's won their biggest-ever peacetime contract, to make lenses for the National Cash Register Company's microprojector. In 1971 they secured a large order for ordnance sights. British design awards went to the M41 microscope in 1971, to the M85/86 scanning microscope in 1975, and to the image-shearing micromeasurement apparatus in 1981. Other safety-at-work awards went to the York factory.

Various reciprocal selling agreements were concluded in the 1970s to increase penetration of the USA, Far Eastern and French markets. In 1972, the South African arm of Vickers Ltd took over Cooke, Troughton & Simms (South Africa). Development work on ordnance sighting and ranging instruments paid off when Cooke's delivered laser rangefinders for the Vickers' tanks being built for the Nigerian government, but in general such orders were slow and protracted. On the civil side, Vickers Instruments designed Fibercheck, a quality-control system for inspection and measurement of optical glass fibres during manufacture. Fibercheck I was produced in 1982, followed by Fibercheck II in 1984. The apparatus sold well to a growing industry that was trying to overcome its technical production problems.

*Display of Cooke theodolites and levels, 1969.*

By 1983 it was evident that a small company such as Vickers Instruments would never be able to defend its position as a manufacturer of optical microscopes against the formidable Japanese competition. The decision was made to reduce the range and leap a generation of product, concentrating on highly sophisticated scientific and defence instrumentation. Vickers already had a foothold in the fast-growing semiconductor market and after substantial market research, it was decided to exploit this. A new development team was recruited to bring electronics and software expertise to Vickers Instruments' traditional skills in optics and mechanics. Backed by government funding of around £1 million, Quaestor, a revolutionary instrument for the measurement of critical dimensions on microchips, was launched in California in 1985. The instrument generated immediate interest, though the first models had some imperfections that needed correction. Quaestor was relaunched in May 1986 and soon became the world leader in its sector in the face of fierce competition from the United States, Germany and Japan. In recognition of the achievements of the development and marketing teams, supported by the workforce, Vickers Instruments received the Queen's Award for Technology and also the Queen's Award for Exports.

By 1988 Vickers Instruments output was concentrated in high-precision measuring apparatus, selling on a world market, and the laser rangefinders, which were of strategic military importance. At this stage the Vickers Group management decided to sell off the business assets and undertaking of Vickers Instruments (York) and the North American branches to subsidiaries of Bio-Rad Laboratories Inc, USA. For the time being, Bio-Rad Micromeasurements continues to manufacture Quaestor at the York factory. The ordnance instruments' side was passed to British Aerospace, to maintain it in British hands.

Thus the history of Cooke, Troughton & Simms was brought to an end.

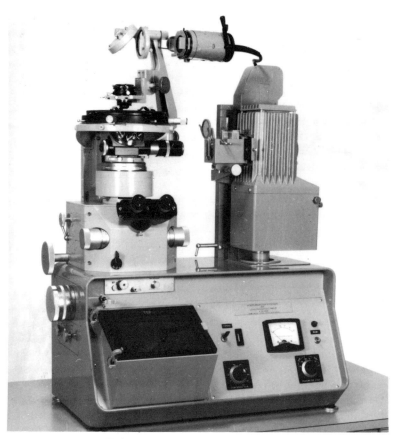

*Vickers Projection Microscope, 1962.*

# *Epilogue* – Looking for Survivors

AN ENORMOUS NUMBER OF FIRST-RATE instruments and apparatus came from the Troughtons, Troughton & Simms, and Cooke's workshops, a more modest number can be attributed to the Simms family and to Vickers Instruments. The purpose of this chapter is to suggest where they might be found today.

Dating has always posed problems, because the signatures are not helpful and, until comparatively recently, only a few major instruments were dated. Alan Stimson showed that the early owners of dividing-engines who were working for the trade put their personal mark on the limbs of instruments that they had divided. The anchor was a favourite symbol, often with initials, but John and Edward Troughton used the plain anchor. Their mark has been found on sextants by other makers, dated between 1795 and 1820. Signatures were examined by Professor Skempton and Joyce Brown, who noted that various styles of the words 'Troughton London' were engraved on instruments made previous to 1825. 'Troughton & Simms' signatures ran for almost a century with little variation and offer no help to dating. But many instruments were not identified: Thomas Cooke was asked to supply some well-known instrument makers and to engrave their names on the instruments. Thus one order instructed him to engrave on a telescope 'L. P. Casella, maker to the Admiralty'. He was similarly instructed to put other names on his levels and on at least one clock. In the later 19th century Troughton & Simms sold many surveying and navigation instruments overseas and these may be identified solely by the trade card of an Australian or other colonial retailer, who probably made himself responsible for any subsequent repairs.

*Cookes' Forth Bridge theodolite, 1884.*

Sales of the more important instruments can often be discovered in the astronomical, engineering, surveying, or other trade journals of the day. References given in earlier chapters will indicate where further information could be sought. Even the humble newspaper can be a source of such information – the York newspapers diligently noted the sales of Cooke's novel or important products.

As working items, many have undergone repairs, modifications and modernisations over the years. The

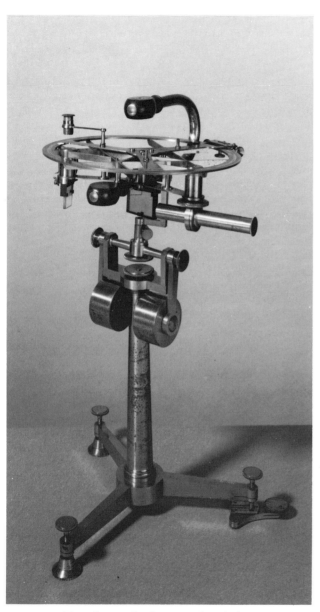

*Troughton reflecting-repeating circle.*

dividing engines of John and Edward Troughton were both 'improved' during their working life, and have been preserved in this modified form. The engine that William Simms made for Hassler underwent significant alteration and has come to rest in the National Museum of American History in Washington. On the astronomical instruments, divisions on silver scales became faint and were re-engraved. Diaphragm webs were replaced or changed to some other type. Telescopes were fitted with photographic lenses, electric drive, and chronograph contacts. In the field or down the mine, lenses, bubbles, compasses or other delicate parts were frequently broken and replaced. Surviving instruments may therefore be composite, from more than one period. Modern conservation also introduces new material which may or may not be identified. The first Troughton mural circle was in a parlous state before its recent conservation for exhibition at the Old Royal Observatory, Greenwich, and has been substantially rebuilt.

Over the centuries much has been lost, but a surprising number of important early pieces survive. Many astronomical instruments have found a home in redundant observatories, now converted to museums. Cooke telescopes and clocks were popular in central Europe, Troughton and Simms supplied instruments to Spain and Italy as well as North America and the former colonies. In the latter 19th century, numerous observatories were equipped with a Troughton & Simms transit circle plus a Cooke telescope. National survey headquarters are similarly disposed to have small museums exhibiting obsolete apparatus. Primary standards of length are generally kept in national laboratories, but in many cities secondary standards can still be found set into walls or pavements for the benefit of local tradesmen.

Whilst a few countries have published national inventories, these may not be exhaustive and can be usefully supplemented by the lists of instruments in astronomical and magnetic observatories that have been published at various times in the past.

Collections of smaller apparatus can be seen in colleges and hospitals, and the houses and observatories of universities and learned societies. Nor should we overlook individual scattered 'open-air' items such as the sundials by Troughton in a Cambridge college and by Cooke in a Yorkshire churchyard, as well as some 12 Cooke turret clocks still in existence.

Apart from national museums with a scientific or technological section, museums of navigation and shipping, and even historic ships, may possess some of the many sextants and station-pointers sold by Troughton & Simms. Railway museums should include the survey equipment that laid the basis of railways across the world. Examples of theodolites said to have belonged to the Brunels and Rennies and other notable engineers may be seen in national and local collections. Theodolites employed on famous structures – the Forth Bridge in Scotland and Sydney Harbour Bridge for example, have survived. Of the engineering products, we have dividing engines made by John and Edward Troughton, William Simms, Thomas Cooke and his sons. These, and a Cooke lathe, are in London's Science Museum.

Sale catalogues of second-hand apparatus and inventories of bequests sometimes allow the history of individual items to be followed from one owner to another over the years. This is particularly the case with prestigious astronomical items bought by wealthy amateurs, for example, Sir Thomas Makdougall Brisbane and Richard Sheepshanks. Items of all types, from the humble set of drawing-instruments to impressive equatorial telescopes, go through the salerooms today and their range and number bears testimony to the output of Cooke, Troughton & Simms and their forbears.

*Cookes' dividing engine, c1868.*

# Further Reading and Notes to the Text

Abbreviations:

## Manuscript sources

AO – Armagh Observatory Archives
APS – American Philosophical Society Archives
BL – British Library Manuscripts
CLRO – City of London Record Office
CUL – Cambridge University Library Manuscripts
CUO – Cambridge University Observatory Archives
GL – Guildhall Library Manuscripts
GLRO – Greater London Record Office
ICE – Institution of Civil Engineers Archives
IOR – India Office Records
LP – Library of Lambeth Palace Manuscripts
MHS – Museum of the History of Science, Oxford
NLS – National Library of Scotland Manuscripts
NRO – Northamptonshire Record Office
PRO – Public Record Office
RAS – Royal Astronomical Society Manuscripts
RGO – Royal Greenwich Observatory Archives
ROE – Royal Observatory Edinburgh Archives
RS – Royal Society Manuscripts
RSA – Royal Society of Arts Manuscripts
SML – Science Museum Library, Archive Collection
SPRI – Scott Polar Research Institute, Cambridge
VI – Vickers Instruments Archive, Borthwick Institute
    (NB – Documents in this archive do not yet
        have a catalogue number.)

## Encyclopedias and Periodicals

EE – Brewster's *Edinburgh Encyclopedia* [undated] to 1830
ESR – *Empire Survey Review*
ILN – *Illustrated London News*
MemRAS – *Memoirs, Royal Astronomical Society*
MNRAS – *Monthly Notices, Royal Astronomical Society*

NRRS – *Notes and Records of the Royal Society of London*
PhTr – *Philosophical Transactions of the Royal Society*
RC – *Rees' Cyclopedia* 1818 etc
PP – denotes Parliamentary Papers.

————

## Prologue: The Business of Instruments

Further reading:

J. A. Bennett, *The Divided Circle*, (London, 1987).
A. J. Turner, *Early Scientific Instruments*, (London, 1987).
M. Daumas, *Scientific Instruments of the 17th and 18th Centuries and their Makers*, (London, 1972).
C. Singer et al, *A History of Technology*, (London, 1958), vol 4, Chapter 12: 'Glass'; Chapter 13: 'Precision mechanics'; Chapter 14: 'Machine tools'.

————

## Chapter 1: At the Sign of the Orrery

Further reading:

W. Pearson, *Introduction to Practical Astronomy*, (London, 1829) 2 vols.
A. Chapman, *Dividing the Circle*, (Chichester, 1990).
R. Porter, S. Schaffer, J. Bennett and O. Brown, *Science and Profit in 18th Century London*, (Cambridge, 1985).
A. N. Stimson, 'Some Board of Longitude instruments in the nineteenth century', in P. R. de Clerq (editor), *Nineteenth Century Scientific Instruments and their Makers*, (Leiden and Amsterdam, 1985).

Notes:

Biographical details from A. W. Skempton and J. Brown, 'John and Edward Troughton' *NRRS* **27** (1973); 233-262, other dates from parish records.

On John Troughton's dividing, see E. Troughton, 'An account of the method of dividing . . .' *PhTr* **99** (1809); 105-154, 'Graduation' RC **16** and 'Graduation' EE **10**.

John Troughton's bank account, 1783-1801, is with Messrs Hoare & Co. The transfer from Cole to Troughton is seen in GL Land Tax Registers, and GL Sun Insurance Policy Registers. The extent of the property occupied by Wright, Cole and Troughton over the years is shown in plans accompanying the leases, now in NRO Church Commissioners Records 116770 to 116782.

On Ramsden's Palermo Circle, 'Circle' EE **6**, with Troughton's opinion of it in his 'Description of a Mural Circle . . .' BL Add 42,076, f97r. On the Coimbra Equatorial, see 'Equatorial' RC **13** and Araujo d'Azevedo, 'Uber die Sternwart zu Coimbra', *Monatliche Correspondenz* **3** (1801); 71. On the Coimbra quadrant see *Mon. Corr.* **3** (1801); 196 and letter from Magellan, 1788, in *Astronomisches Jahrbuch* 1791 (1788); 258. Magellan's payments to Troughton are shown in his account with Messrs Hoare's bank. A description is in 'Astronomical Instruments – Quadrant' EE **2**. On the Armagh equatorial see AO M.51/5, 6, 7 and M.129, and on its defects, E. Troughton, 'On Mural Circles . . .' BL Add 42,076 f97r. The Observatory's history is in J. A. Bennett, *Church, State and Astronomy: 200 Years of Astronomy at Armagh*, (Armagh, 1990). On the Board of Longitude, its instruments and Troughton invoices etc, see principally Acts, Orders etc, RGO 14/1, f160; Confirmed Minutes, 14/7, 14/8, 14/13, and Nevil Maskelyne, Memorandum Books VI and VII, Wiltshire Record Office (copies with RGO). On the station pointer see *Nautical Magazine* 1842; 258, on the dip sector, RGO 14/7 ff32-3, 40, 45. Remarks about Troughton instruments abound in R. H. Phillmore, *Historical Records of the Survey of India*, notably **1**, (Dehra Dun, 1945); 202, and **2** (1950); 191, 198, 223, 252. See also R. H. Colebrook, 'Astronomical Observations . . .' *Asiatick Researches* **4** (1801); 133, W. Lambton, 'Account of a method . . .' *Ibid* **7** (1803); 312-335, and W. Hunter, 'Astronomical Observations . . .', IOR E/4/892, p594.

Many passing references to Troughton instruments in Europe occur in early numbers of *Astronomisches Jahrbuch* (Berlin), *Monatliche Correspondenz* (Gotha), and *Allgemeine Geographische Ephemeriden* (Weimar), notably E. Troughton, letter to von Zach, 1800, in *Mon. Corr.* **2** (1800); 207-222 and 531. On von Brühl's circle, see H. M. de Brühl, *On Astronomical Circles*, (London, 1794), 'Circle' EE **6**, and von Zach, 'Ueber die untersuchung astronomische Kreise . . .', *Archiv der Mathematik* (Leipzig) **1** (1795); 258-9. On Lee's circle, see 'Capt. Smyth's account of his observatory at Bedford', *MemRAS* **4** (1828-31); 545-568. On the Troughton reflecting circle, see Edward Troughton, 'A comparison of the repeating circle . . .' *MemRAS* **1** (1822); 33-54, and 'Circle' EE **6**.

Troughton's observatory is described in W. Simms, *The Achromatic Telescope*, (London, 1852); 64-66, his observations of the Transit of Mercury are in *All. Geog. Eph.* **4** (1799); 172, its lat. and long. in *Mon. Corr.* **2** (1800); 222.

Apprenticeship records have been supplied or confirmed from Project SIMON.

On Rehe, Fayrer and the cutting-engine, see 'Cutting engine' RC **10** and 'Equatorial' RC **13**, also Pearson, *Introduction to Practical Astronomy*, **2** (1829); 464-472, and J. Fayrer, 'Three-wheeled clock', *Transactions of the Society of Arts* **37** (1820); 138-146. For John Troughton's membership of the Society of Civil Engineers, see ICE, Society of Civil Engineers, 2nd Minute Book 1793-1821.

Assessment of John Troughton's estate is in PRO, IR 26/125, Reg. 371.

---

**Chapter 2: Master of His Craft**

Further reading:

W. Pearson, *Introduction to Practical Astronomy*, (London, 1829) 2 vols.

D. Howse, *Royal Greenwich Observatory vol. 3. Its Buildings and Instruments.* (London, 1975).

Notes:

For styles of Troughton bill-heads, see Board of Longitude Accounts, RGO 14/18. On the Leipzig circle, see Troughton's letter to von Zach, 1800, *Mon. Corr.* **2** (1800); 221, for another consignment in 1801, Troughton's letter to von Zach, *ibid* **5** (1802); 358-362. On Troughton observatory instruments, see A. Hanle and O. Mittlestaedt, 'Die Sternwarte auf dem kleine Seeberg bei Gotha', *Sterne und Weltraum* **2** (1977); 43-46, and P. Brosche, 'Gotha und der Seeberg', *ibid* **7-8** (1988); 423-427; P. Müürsepp, 'Die alte Sterwarte in Tartu' (ie, Dorpat), *ibid* **6** (1966); 129-131. Prices of the small and medium instruments are from *Astr. Jahrb.* 1803 (1800); 245-6, *ibid* 1806 (1803); 262, *ibid* 1808 (1805); 195, *Mon. Corr.* **5** (1802); 358-362.

On standards of length see G. Shuckburgh, 'An account of some endeavours to ascertain a standard of weight and measure' *PhTr* **88** (1798); 133-182, on the Aberdeen measure, J. S. Reid, 'Patrick Copland 1748-1822 . . .', *Aberdeen University Review* **51** (1985); 231-4, which notes the bill dated 1802. (Some sources give other dates for this measure, which is now lost.) On Pictet, see M. A. Pictet, *Voyage de Trois Mois en Angleterre, . . . en 1801,* (Geneva, 1802); 301-2 and his 'Comparaison du mètre definitif . . .' *Bibliothèque Britannique* **19** (1802); 109-222. For Hassler's scale see F. R. Hassler, 'Papers on various subjects . . . 1824', *Transactions, American Philosophical Society* **2** (1825); 246-7, and his *Comparison of Weights and Measures,* (Washington, 1832); 21-22. For the OS and RAS scales see infra, Chapter 4.

Josiah Dancer's work for Troughton is spoken of on p3 of 'J. B. Dancer, an Autobiographical Sketch', *Manchester Memoirs* **107** (1964-5); 1-28. On the younger Fayrer, see Troughton's letters to Thomas Young, 1820, in RGO 14/48 f198 and f200, and B. Warner, *Astronomers at the Cape,* (Capetown, 1979); 12-13. For Troughton's other journeymen, see the biography of Barrow in R. H. Phillimore, *Historical Records of the Survey of India* **4** (Dehra Dun, 1958); 417-419, for Yeates, his obituary in MNRAS **37** (1877); 159-60, for Drechsler, see *Astr. Jahr.* 1808 (1805); 275 and *Mon. Corr.* **5** (1802); 358-362.

Proposals for the mural circle, 1807 are in RS Minutes of Council VII, p498 and pp503-4, Edward Troughton's paper 'Description of a mural circle etc' is BL Add 42,076, ff94-109. The model is mentioned in 'Circle' p485, EE **6**. Donkin's part in building this and other instruments is touched on in The Bryan Donkin Co, *A Brief Account of Bryan Donkin FRS, . . .* (Privately published, 1953). On platinum for graduated circles, see J. A. Chaldecott, 'Platinum and palladium in astronomy and navigation', *Platinum Metals Review* **31** (1987); 91-100.

Troughton's letter to Maskelyne, 1808, RS M.1.35 accompanied his paper 'Account of a method of dividing . . .' *PhTr* **99** (1809); 105-145, abstracted in 'Graduation EE **10**, especially pp353-7, and 'Graduation' RC. Troughton's certificate of election to the American Philosophical Society is in APS. On his election to the Royal Society of Edinburgh, the proposal, 1821, is NLS Acc 10,000/43 and his admission, 1822, is noted in Minutes Book of the RSE, NLS Acc 10,000/4. VI holds his Clockmakers Freedom Certificate. The RAS holds records of his election to the RAS and his attendances at its Dining Club. Other social invitations are noted in, to Maskelyne, 1808, 'Dinner dates 1804-10', Maskelyne Memo. Book XI, Wiltshire Record Office, to Abraham Robertson, 1810 and 1814, RAS Radcliffe B 2.49 and B 2.56, to South, at Passy, 1824, RS M 1.136, to Paris, RAS Radcliffe B 2.60. Goods ordered by Dunlop in 1805, APS mss Coll.

On Hassler's visit see F. Cajori, *The Chequered Career of F. R. Hassler,* (Boston, Mass, 1929), F. R. Hassler, *Principal Documents . . .* **3** (New York, 1834); 28, 30, 67-8 etc. His 'Papers on various subjects', *Trans. Amer. Phil. Soc.* **2** (1825); 246-7, Troughton's letter to Robertson, 1814, RAS Radcliffe B 2.56. For Hassler's subsequent visit and purchases, see infra, Chapter 4.

Troughton's views on chronometers are in RGO 14/27 f272. For his pendulum see 'Description of a tubular pendulum', *Nicholson's Journal* **9** (1804);

225- 30 and W. H. Smyth, *Cycle of Celestial Objects*, (London, 1860); 123. On the nautical top, see 'Sextant p70', EE **18**, W. H. Smyth, *Cycle of Celestial Objects*, (London, 1860); 15. Letter, Troughton to Robertson, 1814, RAS Radcliffe B 2.57, J. Ross, A voyage of discovery . . . 1818, (London, 1819) **2**; 225, 'The Nautical Top', Stokes papers, CUL Add 7656, TR 136, N. Reingold (ed), *The Papers of Joseph Henry*, (Washington, 1972) **3**; 458. Troughton's barometers are described in 'Barometer', RC. Pistor's price-list is in *Annalen der Physik* (1814); 227-8. Troughton's level is in 'Surveying' RC. For the Greenwich instruments see D. Howse, *Greenwich Observatory: 3, The Instruments*, (London, 1975). On adjustments and repairs, see RGO 5/73, ff25-27, RGO 5/77, [unf] 4 Aug. 1827, RGO 5/13, ff9, 10, 12, 15. For Troughton's invoice for a transit sold to Mudge see letter, Colby to R. H. Crew, 1820, in PRO OS 3/260, ff81-2. On the base-measuring apparatus, see W. Yolland, *An Account of the Measurement of the Loch Foyle Base*, (London, 1847).

———

## Chapter 3: William Simms

Further reading:

C. Close, *A History of the Ordnance Survey*, (Chatham, 1926).

M. C. Donnelly, *A Short History of Observatories*, (Oregon, 1973).

R. H. Phillimore, *Historical Records of the Survey of India*, **4**, 1830-43: Sir George Everest, (Dehra Dun, 1958).

W. A. Seymour (ed), *A History of the Ordnance Survey*, (Folkestone, 1980).

Notes:

For Simms family history see E. J. Mennim, *Reid's Heirs*, (Braunston, 1989); corrected and supplemented from parish registers and PO Directories. An excellent description of the industrial Birmingham where metal-working craftsmen such as the Simms family were able to

prosper, and its contrast to London, is Eric Hopkins, *Birmingham, The First Manufacturing Town in the World*, 1760-1840, (London, 1989).

'William's own statement' here and later, comes from Simms' Dividing Notebook, 1824-38, VI. For the protractor sent to the Society of Arts, see RSA F1/177 and Minutes of Committees 1816-17, pages 232, 269 and 275. On the London Mechanics Institute etc, see T. Kelly, *George Birkbeck, Pioneer of Adult Education*, (London, 1957). Simms family and other attendances at the LMI are from its Registers, held at Birkbeck College.

Pearson's acquisition of the St Petersburg circle is in W. Pearson, *Introduction to Practical Astronomy*, **2** (London, 1829); 434, the 10-years' delay is mentioned in a letter, Dollond to Lee, 1844, LP mss 2878 f147. Troughton referred to his travels in France in letters, to Robertson, 1824, RAS Radcliffe B 2.60, and to South, 1825, RS M.1.136. Negotiations for the Edinburgh instruments are in ROE Edinburgh Astronomical Institution, Minute Book **1** (1811-31) and **2** (1831-47). See also Simms' Dividing Notebook; 8.

Construction and comparisons of OS bars are taken from W. Yolland, *An Account of the Measurement of the Loch Foyle Base*, (London, 1847). There are voluminous Everest papers in IOR L/MIL/5 No. 248 Coll. 205, with references to other files, and in *Great Trigonometrical Survey of India* Reports, some by subject, others by date. On Gravatt's level, made by T & S, see ICE Minutes of Conversations **3**, Meeting of 26 May 1835 No. 17; 3-8.

F. W. Simms' books are: *Treatise on the Principal Mathematical Instruments Employed in Surveying, Levelling and Astronomy*, (London, first edition 1834, Spanish edition Cadiz, 1846, several American editions published at Baltimore); *Treatise on the Principal Mathematical Drawing Instruments Employed by the Engineer, Architect and Surveyor*, (London, first edition 1837); *Treatise on the Principles and Practise of Levelling*, (London, first edition 1837).

M. Hoskin and others have re-examined the South affair in 'Astronomers at war: South *v* Sheepshanks', and 'More on South and Sheepshanks . . .' *Journal for the History of Astronomy,* **20**(1), (1989); 175-212 and *ibid* **22**(2), (1991), 174-9. The equatorial bought from Huddart is described in *PhTr* **114**, (1824); 4-11. William Simms' account of events is in William Simms' '. . . diary entries . . . re James South' in VI. Edward Troughton's estate was analysed in PRO IR 26/1400 Reg. 427. VI has 'Fayrer's case'. The British Library has Sotheby's sale catalogue of Troughton's effects, annotated with buyers and prices, shelf-mark S-CS 206(8).

---

## Chapter 4: Standards of Precision

Further reading:

G. B. Airy, *The Autobiography of Sir George Airy,* (Cambridge, 1896).

R. D. Connor, *The Weights and Measures of England,* (London, 1987).

D. Howse, *Greenwich Time and the Discovery of Longitude,* (Oxford, 1980).

W. Simms, *The Achromatic Telescope and its Various Mountings, Especially the Equatorial,* (London, 1852).

Notes:

Simms' address to the Civil Engineers on dividing, on 6 May 1834, was recorded in ICE Minutes of Conversation, **2**, No. 106. The engine was described in W. H. Simms, 'On a self-acting circular dividing engine', *MNRAS* **5** (1939-43); 291-2, and *MRAS* **15** (1846); 83-90.

Parish duties are from St Bride's Vestry Minutes, GL 6554/10, as is the collapse of 137-8 Fleet Street, also reported in *The Times,* 1 March 1841 p5e. The Vestry Minutes record subsequent events. Insurance policy for the completed buildings is in GL 6636.

On the Hassler theodolite exhibited, see letter, Blunt to Hassler, 1836, in Hassler, *Principal Documents* **3**; 16. The dividing engine is described in *J. Franklin Inst.* **12** (1846); 258-61 and *Proc. Amer. Phil. Soc.* **4**

(1845); 160. For Wilkes, see J. D. Borthwick, 'Outfitting the US Exploring Expedition . . .', *Proc. Amer. Phil. Soc.* **109** (1965); 159-172. Loomis' instruments for Ohio are described in C. André and A. Angot, *L'astronomie Practique et les Observatoires* **3**, (Paris, 1877). Montojo's apparatus is on pp151-3 of Simms' Technical Notebook, (1839-1901) in VI. For Folque at T & S, see pp119-120 in the 'Diario de Felipe Folque, 1854' transcribed in *Revista do Instituto geográfico e cadastral,* No. 6 (1986); 113-132.

Gilbert's displacement as EIC supplier is chronicled in IOR P/36/28 No. 15, 117 & 119, and E/4/759; 198-9. Hodgson's collaboration with Simms is told in J. A. Hodgson, 'Memorandum of the differences of the meridian of the Observatory at Madras', *J. Asiatic Soc.* **9** (1840); 75-90. Theodolites sent out in Waugh's time are described in *Great Trigonometrical Survey, Records,* **2**; 51 and Appendix 2; 15-31.

On railways, see G. Biddle, *The Railway Surveyors,* (London, 1990). Comparisons of the RAS standard, made at the Houses of Parliament, are described in RAS 71; 30-1. The Commission on standards reported in PP 1842 (356)XXV.263. Airy's voluminous papers are in RGO 6/350-356. He summarised its work in G. B. Airy, 'Account of the construction of the new national standards of length and of its principal copies', *PhTr* **147** (1857); 621-702.

On astronomical instruments sent overseas: Brussels, see J. Perrotin, *Visite à Divers Observatoires D'Europe,* (Paris, 1881), Simms' Dividing Notebook; 63 and the anniversary volume of *Bull. Astronomique* **10**(1) 1985. The Brussels equatorial is fig. 142 of J. A. Repsold, *Zur Geschichte der Astronomischen Messwerkzeuge,* **2** (Leipzig, 1914). For Lucknow, see *MNRAS* **11** (1850-51); 90-4. On Simms' part in the Northumberland telescope, see *Report of the [Cambridge] University Syndicate* for 1837, 1838, 1839. The telescope itself was described by G. B. Airy, *Account of the Northumberland Equatorial and Dome, attached to Cambridge University,* (Cambridge, 1844). On the rebuilding of Bird's transit, see N. D. Thackeray, *The Radcliffe Observatory,* (Cambridge, 1972). On 'The Liverpool equatorial' see *Hermes* **14**(5), (1967); 155-8. On West Point, Harvard,

Tuscaloosa, and Georgetown, see C . André and A. Angot, *L'astronomie Practique et les Observatoires* **3**, (Paris, 1877). Simms visit to Paris is reported in his Technical Notebook; 64. On his Harvard instruments, see B. Z. Jones, 'Diary of the two Bonds, 1846-9, first Directors of the Harvard College Observatory', *Harvard Library Bulletin* **15** (1967); 368-386 and *ibid,* **16** (1968); 49-71 and 178-207.

Simms' refusal to make a dividing engine for the EIC is IOR E/4/815; 274-5. T & S exhibits in the 1851 Exhibition are in *Great Exhibition of the Works of all Nations,* Catalogue (1851); . . ., with comments by J. Drew, 'On the astronomical instruments in the Great Exhibition', *Civil Engineer and Architect's Journal* **14** (1851); 435-7. On the elliptograph, see RGO 6/451 ff66r to 81r. The construction of Airy's 1847 altazimuth and 1850 transit can be traced through correspondence in RGO 6/720, /723 and elsewhere in RGO class 6; their descriptions in G. B. Airy, 'Description of the Transit Circle', *Astronomical Observations 1852,* Appendix, and *ibid* 1847; iv-xxvii. Correspondence concerning details of the 1851 zenith and the 1859 equatorial are in appropriate parts of RGO 6 and formally described by Airy in *Astronomical Observations 1854,* Appendix 1, and *ibid* 1868, Appendix 3.

----

**Chapter 5: Surveying the World**

Further reading:

J. A. Bennett, *Science at the Great Exhibition,* (Cambridge, 1983).

J. A. Bennett, *The Celebrated Phenomena of Colours: The Early History of the Spectroscope,* (Cambridge, 1984).

M. E. W. Williams, 'Astronomy in London 1860-1900', *Quarterly Journal, Royal Astronomical Society* **28** (1987); 10-26.

Notes:

For the history of optical glass see J. F. Chance, *A History of the Firm of Chance Brothers & Co.,* (London, 1919); 171-186. William Simms' interest is shown by his 'On the manufacture of optical glass in England', *MNRAS* **9** (1848-9); 147-8.

On the India Store Observatory, see R. J. Mann, 'The Lambeth Observatory', *Quarterly Journal of Science* **6** (1869); 342-352. Strange's discussions on the theodolite are in IOR L/MIL/2/1543 letters 1067 and 1125, L/MIL/2/1545 Letter 1563 and L/MIL/2/1558 Letter 4179. His published description is 'A great new theodolite', *Proceedings of the Royal Society* **20** (1872); 317-328. On its arrival in South Africa, see D. Gill, *History and Description of the Royal Observatory, Cape of Good Hope,* (London, 1913); xliii-xliv.

Simms letter to Challis on mural circles is CUO Letters 1860/32. On the Sheepshanks bequest, see 'Obituary, Miss Ann Sheepshanks', *MNRAS* **37** (1876-7); 143-145. Examples of Airy advising on instrument makers are in RGO 6, eg, to Cranch, RGO 6/159. Harvard opinions of Simms are from B. Z. Jones, *The Harvard College Observatory, 1839-1919,* (Harvard, 1971); especially pp142, 146, 152. The Simms letter which annoyed Piazzi Smyth is ROE C. P. Smyth Diaries XXVII, 1875 July 14. David Gill's correspondence with Troughton & Simms is scattered through the ROE Dunecht Letters-in and Letters-out for the years 1871-3. Instruments for the Mexican observatories are described by A. Anguiano, *Primera Memoria del Observatorio Astronómico Nacional Establecido en Chapultepec,* (Mexico, 1880); 14-15, 19-21 and RGO 6/177, f167. W. Simms' daughter expressed her opinion of James Simms in her letter to Gunther, MHS Gunther 59.

PRO Works 20/2-3 refers to emplacement of the Trafalgar Square standards; that of the Guildhall standards is in CRO Minutes, Sub-Cttee City Lands, 26 June 1877 and J. J. Baddeley, *The Guildhall of the City of London,* (London, 1939); 50. A zenith telescope for India (see illus.) was described in *Great Trigonometrical Survey,* **18**, 'Observations for Latitude, 1885-1905', (Dehra Dun, 1906); 16.

Equipment taken for the Transit of Venus is described in G. B. Airy, *Account of Observations of the Transit of Venus, 1874,* (London, 1881); 9-10, passim.

Instruments for the City & Guilds Institute are mentioned in A. E. Tutton, 'An instrument for grinding section-plates and prisms of crystals . . .' and 'An instrument of precision for producing monochromatic light . . .', *PhTr A* **185**, (1894); 887-912 and 913-941, and H. A. Meiers, 'A students' goniometer', *Mineral Magazine* **9** (1890-91); 214-216.

A. J. Winterhalter described the Charlton Works in pp178-9 of Appendix I to *Washington Naval Observatory, Observations [for] 1885,* (Washington, 1891). On Troughton's dividing engine working till 1920, see *Optical Convention of 1926, Catalogue*; 289 (London, 1926).

A. H. Marindin's Patent is No. 16,647 of 1901, 'A cheap portable rangefinder with end prisms of reflecting half-images adjustable by micrometer'. For its description and use as issued, see *Handbook of the Rangefinder Infantry No. 1 (Marindin) 1913,* (HMSO, War Office).

---

## Chapter 6: The Self-Made Man

Further reading:

C. Feinstein (ed), *The British Association, York, 1831-1981,* (York, 1982).

Notes:

Thomas Cooke's early life is recounted in S. Smiles, *Men of Invention and Industry,* (London, 1884); 336-348 and in his obituary, *MNRAS* **29**, (1868); 130-135. Notices and advertisements appeared in *Yorkshire Gazette,* 4 March and 26 August 1837, 9 March 1844, 27 January 1849. John Scott described Cooke's early business life in *YG,* 7, 14, 21 February and 7 March 1925. VI holds his Order Book for 1856-68.

For the Paris Exhibition, see *Exposition Universelle de 1855, Rapports du Jury Mixte International,* (Paris, 1861); I, 400. For the London Exhibition, *International Exhibition, 1862, Medals and Honourable Mentions,* (London, 1862); 197 and 211 and *Practical Mechanic's Journal Record of the Great Exhibition, 1862*; 498, 514-5, 519. Cooke's contribution to the Yorkshire Exhibition of 1857 is given in *YG,* 6 August 1857; 2a, that for the 1866 Yorkshire Exhibition, in *YG,* 6 October 1866; 5d-e. VI holds the 'List of journeys of the Steam-carriage'.

On Cooke's turret clocks, see also *National Encyclopedia* **7**, article 'Horology', (Glasgow, 1867-8); 462. The Prince Consort's telescope is described in *Yorkshire Herald,* 23 June 1860; 5b-c.

On the Newall telescope, see *Nature* **1** (1870); 408-410. On its clock regulator and micrometer illumination, 'The new telescope at Eton', *ibid*; 263-264, and *Engineer,* **29** (1870); 289. D. W. Dewhirst, 'The Newall telescope', *J British Astronomical Association,* **80** (6), (1970); Historical section, 493-495, presents an impartial retrospective.

Strange's report on Cooke and his establishment is IOR L/E/3/198; pp657-663. The defective theodolites are discussed in IOR L/E/3/198; p7, pp28-31. On the transits, see two papers by A. Strange, 'On an aluminium bronze transit axis', *MNRAS* **25** (1865); 177-82 and 'On a transit and zenith sector', *Proceedings of the Royal Society,* **15** (1867); 385-7. A. Yeates commented 'On the . . . bearings for the pivots of transit instruments', *MNRAS* **25** (1864-5); 214. On their employment, *Great Trigonometrical Survey of India,* **9**, *Electro-telegraphic operations,* (Dehra Dun, 1883); xiii-xvii + 1-4.

---

## Chapter 7: Buckingham Works

Further reading:

H. C. King, *The History of the Telescope,* (London, 1955; repr. New York, 1979).

Notes:

*The London Gazette,* 28 October 1879, p6139

records the 'special resolution for liquidation' against the Cooke family. James Wigglesworth's obituary in *MNRAS* **49** (1888-9); 169 refers to his friendship with Cooke. His Will, proved 11 July 1888, mentions his acquisition of Buckingham Works and his offer to sell it.

H. W. Vallé's claim to have worked for Cooke is on the title page of his *The Transit Theodolite . . .* (Brisbane, 1921). C. L. Berger's claim is on piii of his *Manual . . .* (Boston, 1926).

Reports on the levels sent to India are from IOR L/E/3/200. For a list of the precise levels employed at this time, see *Great Trigonometrical Survey of India,* **19**, *Levels of precision 1858-1909,* (Dehra Dun, 1910); 25. On the Forth Bridge instruments, see 'Triangulation and measurement of the Forth Bridge', *The Engineer* **62** (1886); 281, 299, 339.

For astronomical instruments, Adelaide, *South Australia Intelligence Bulletin, Part 2: Adelaide Observatory,* (Adelaide, 1910); Rio, *Engineering* **58** (1894); 661-665 and H. Morize, *Observatório Astronômico, um Sécola de Historia, 1827-1927,* (Rio, 1989), 128-130, 132, 142, 147, 149-50; Uccle, A. J. Winterhalter, p193 in Appendix I of *Washington Naval Observatory, Observations [for] 1885,* (Washington, 1891); Liège, *ibid*, 198-9 and 'A new Belgian Observatory', *The Observatory* **9**, (1886); 206. Winterhalter described Pola in 183-4 of his Appendix . . ., others listed in (eg) P. Stroobant, *Les Observatoires Astronomiques,* (Brussels, 1907). Negotiations for the Greenwich dome are in RGO 6/179, details of the 1893 dome are in W. H. M. Christie, 'On a new dome to be erected at the Royal Observatory, Greenwich', *MNRAS* **51** (1890-91); 436-8.

Sale of the 'Japanese' equatorial, described in *The Engineer* **32** (1871); 322, was noted in E. G. Allingham, *Romance of the Rostrum,* (London, 1924); 73. Piazzi Smyth's correspondence is in ROE Archive A.13-58, 15-71 and 120. Cooke's entries in the Vienna Exhibition are listed in *The British Section at the Vienna Exhibition, 1873, Official Catalogue* (2nd ed. London, 1874); 106.

Details of Cooke's financial situation are from the Board Minutes of the Yorkshire Banking Company, in the archives of Midland Bank Group.

Buckingham Works in 1894 was described in *Engineering* **58** (1894); 660-1, with reports of its productions, 661-3, 696.

On Watkin's rangefinders, PP 1888 (235) LXV.417 contains the Treasury Minute relating to his award. The depression rangefinder is described in *Encyclopedia Britannica*, 11th ed. article 'Rangefinder'. For the Mekometer, see *Handbook of the Mekometer,* (HMSO, 1911).

Bolton's level is patent No. 17,858 of 1893. For Thomas Cushing's level, see his booklet *On a New Form of Levelling Instrument,* (London, 1879). John Fergusson's percentage theodolite, Patent No. 25,267 of 1898, was described in his booklet *Fergusson's Surveying Circle and Percentage Tables,* (London, 1901).

Biographical material on H. Dennis Taylor comes from obituaries in *Proceedings of the Physical Society of London* **55** (1943); 508-511; *Photographic Journal* **83** (1943); 160; *Nature* **151** (1943); 442-3, and from 'Award of the Duddell medal, 1934 . . .' *Proc. Phys. Soc.* **46** (1934); 897-8 and pp563-4 in E. W. Taylor's obituary in *Biographical Notices of Fellows of the Royal Society,* (1980); 563-577. On the temperature-compensated cell, see D. W. Dewhirst, 'A Cooke photovisual lens in a compensated cell', *Sky and Telescope,* (January 1975); 24-5. The first three editions of *The Adjustment and Testing of Telescope Objectives* were published by T. Cooke & Sons, the 4th edition was published by Grubb, Parsons & Co., Newcastle, with a new Chapter 14, 'The Cooke photovisual objective' and Taylor's papers from *MNRAS* **54**(2), (5) and *MRAS* **51** as Appendixes A, B, and C.

---

## Chapter 8: Changing Horizons

Further reading:

R. P. T. Davenport-Hines, 'Vickers as a multinational before 1945', pp43-74 in G. Jones (ed), *British Multinationals, Origins, Management and Performance,* (Business History Series, Aldershot, 1986).

G. Hartcup, *The War of Invention: Scientific Developments, 1914-18*, (London, 1988).

J. T. Sumida, *In Defence of Naval Supremacy*, (Boston, 1989).

Notes:

Architects' drawings of Buckingham Works showing the turn-of-century and WW1 expansions are in the Atkinson-Brierley papers, Borthwick Institute.

H. A. Denholm Fraser described the Cooke magnetometer in 'The unifilar magnetometer of the magnetic survey of India' *Terrestrial magnetism and atmospheric electricity* **6** (1901); 65-69 and in *Survey of India Professional Papers* **8**, (Dehra Dun, 1901). The US Coast Survey models are illustrated in R. P. Multhauf and G. Good, *A Brief History of Geomagnetism*, (Washington, 1987) figures 50 and 74, (the caption errs in giving its date of development as 1906 and its place of manufacture as London). See also Cookes' catalogue of 1902, *Surveying Instruments*.

Correspondence with Cooke's about the instruments for the Antarctic Expedition is in SPRI ms 280/28/6: British Antarctic Survey Expedition 1910-13, vol 6, Section 0, file 537: 16, 17, 18, 21, and a letter, Wright to Debenham, 1919, [no file number]. The published descriptions are by F. Debenham, in the volume 'Reports on the maps and surveys'; 4-7, in *The British Terra Nova Expedition*, (London, 1923). See also *Vickers News* **2**(18), (1920).

Jeffcott's tacheometer, Patent No. 18,721 of 1912, was described by him in *Transactions of the Institute of Civil Engineers of Ireland* **41** (1915); 48-87. See also *Journal of Scientific Instruments* **3** (1925-6); 509. The Sydney Harbour Bridge level is mentioned in *Yorkshire Gazette*, 4 April 1925.

The Brazilian telescope is described in *Engineering* **115** (1923); 130-1, 161-2, 223-5, and *Yorkshire Gazette*, 2 and 9 February 1923. The Greenwich transit is described in D. Howse, *Greenwich Observatory* **3** (1975); 48-51, and *Vickers News*, July 1937.

On Pollen, the Argo Company, and dealings with Cooke's, see A. Pollen, *The Great Gunnery Scandal*,

(London, 1980) and J. T. Sumida (ed), *The Pollen Papers*, (Naval Records Society Pub. No. 124, 1984). Brief references giving Cooke's and Vickers' view are in CUL Vickers 57.24/8; Vickers 771.53-D-Z (1959); Vickers 618, and VI, Directors' Minute Book. These accounts differ on certain points. For outside assessments, see Hartcup and Sumida (Further Reading, this Chapter). Financial rewards are in PP 1924-5, Cmnd 2275, ix 225, '3rd Report, Royal Commission on Awards to Inventors', Claimant 282 and in Appendix, Claimant 3, and PP 1926 Cmnd 2625, viii 319, '4th Report . . .', Claimant 351. E. W. Taylor's paper 'The Cooke-Pollen rangefinder' was published first in *Journal of the US Artillery* **41**(3), (1914); 295-310 and reprinted in *Journal, American Society of Naval Engineers* **26** (1914); 813-831. See also H. D. Taylor's Patents 13,562 of 1907 and 20,315 of 1908.

*The History of the Ministry of Munitions* **11**, (London, 1922), pt III, deals with optical munitions and is complemented by R. and K. Macleod, 'Government and the optical industry in Britain, 1914-18', pp165-203 in J. M. Winter (ed), *War and Economic Development*, (Cambridge, 1975). Twyman wrote of his dealings with Cooke's and Vickers in his autobiography, in SML Hilger archive 3/1.

On E. Wilfred Taylor, see *Biographical Notices of Fellows of the Royal Society* (1980); 563-577 (which has a Bibliography) and obituary in *The Times*, 8 November 1980; 16g.

--------

## Chapter 9: Under Vickers' Control

Notes:

VI has Board Minute Books for the years 1925 to 1963 and records of the liquidation of 1924. See also Companies' Winding-up Papers, PRO J.13, No. 10416.

Events surrounding the development of the Tavistock theodolite may be found in E. R. L. Peake, 'The Tavistock theodolite', *Geographical Journal* **73** (1929); 513-528; W. H. Connell, 'The Tavistock theodolite', *Canadian Surveyor* **3**(10) (1930); 7-11; G. Cheetham,

'The Tavistock theodolite', *Geog. J.* **77** (1931); 442-454; T. Y. Baker, 'The Tavistock theodolite', *South African Survey Journal* **4** (1934); 216-219; 'Colonel Spring' (pseud.), 'Jottings – the Tavistock', *ESR* **5** (1939-40); 304-307; E. W. Taylor, 'The new geodetic Tavistock theodolite', *ESR* **6** (1941-2); 69-75, 225-269, 393-401, 455-462. The patent is T. Y. Baker and R. W. Cheshire, No. 288,416 of 1927. For the Tavistock's reception in South Africa, see T. Y. Baker, 'The Tavistock Theodolite', *S. A. Surv. J.* **4** (1931-6); 168-172 and 216-219.

The universal milling and shaping machine was described in *Journal of Scientific Instruments* **4** (1926-7); 488-491. 'Notices – the division errors of a graduated circle', *ESR* **2** (1933); 191, comments on the accuracy then obtained. Cooke exhibits at the 1926 Optical Convention are in the *Catalogue . . .* (Optical Convention, London, 1926); 70, 168, 213-222, 263. See also W. H. Connell, 'The Heape and Grylls machine for high speed photography', *J. Sci. Insts.* **4** (1926-7); 82-7.

On the effects of the Safeguarding of Industries Act, 1921, see PP 'Report of a Committee appointed by the Board of Trade . . .' 1926 Cmnd 2631, xv.

W. H. Connell's sales reports are in VI. Among his 'publicity' articles are 'Surveying instruments', *Canadian Surveyor* **3**(8) (1930); 3, 5-7; 'Instructions for the care and maintenance of instruments', *Can. Surv.* **3**(12) (1931); 17-19; 'Some recent improvements in the design and construction of British made surveying instruments' *Proceedings, South Wales Institute of Engineers* **39**(1) (1923); 43-56; 'The renaissance of British instrument making', *Instrument World* **1**(6) (1928); 165-172; 'Some recent developments in the design and construction of surveying instruments', *Instr. W.* **2**(23) (1930); 165-172. The South American tour generated articles in *Anales del Instituto de Ingenieros de Chile*, February 1929; *Revista Brasiliera de Engenharia* **21** (1931); 149-154 and 192-4, and *La Ingeniería* **36** (1932); 47-55. Connell put very similar articles into the Australian and South African surveying journals.

The British Industries fair in Buenos Aires featured in *Engineering* **131** (1931); 317-9. Cookes' publicity is in *Buenos Aires, Exposición Britanica de Artes e Industrías 1931 – Catálogo Oficial*, (Buenos Aires, 1931) unp. The British Industries Fair in Birmingham was the subject of a Supplement of 24 May, in *The Engineer* **159** (1935); i-iii.

Progress in the years from 1932 is charted in Cooke, Troughton & Simms, Quarterly Reports, CUL Vickers 167 seriatim. The British Association visit to Cookes' factory is briefly mentioned in *Report of the British Association for the Advancement of Science* (1932), Appendix, 87-88.

———

**Chapter 10: Short Focus, Wide Field**

Further reading:

B. Bracegirdle, 'Light microscopy, 1865-1985', *Microscopy* **36** (1989); 193-209.

Notes:

This chapter leans heavily on the Cooke, Troughton & Simms, Quarterly Reports, September 1945 to September 1961, CUL Vickers 218 to 282, the Vickers Ltd Chairman's Reports, 1955 to 1987, and not least on reminiscences of former employees and managers of the company. VI has correspondence on the use of the 'Cooke' trademark. For their visit to Cooke's factory, see p248 of 'Conference of Commonwealth Survey Officers, 1947', *ESR* **9** (1948); 186-195 and 248-259.

For a local view of post-war Cooke's, see *Yorkshire Herald*, 13 February 1948, 6c-e. Detailed accounts of C T & S microscope production are B. O. Payne, *Microscope Design and Construction*, (York, 1954) and A. J. Munro, 'A history of Vickers Instruments' microscopes', *Microscopy* **34** (1980); 81-101 and 162-184. The origins of Francis Smith's interference microscope were recounted by K. F. A. Ross on pp110-1 in 'Phase contrast and interference microscopy' *Microscopy* **36** (1988); 97-123.

## Epilogue: Looking for Survivors

Further reading:

H. D. Howse, 'The Greenwich List of Observatories: a world list of astronomical observatories, instruments and clocks, 1670-1850'. *Journal for the History of Astronomy,* **17**(4) (1986); 51pp (dedicated volume).

H. D. Howse, 'The Royal Astronomical Society instrument collection, 1827-1985'. *Quarterly Journal, Royal Astronomical Society,* **27** (1986); 212-236.

H. D. Howse, *Royal Greenwich Observatory: 3. Its Buildings and Instruments,* (London, 1975).

'Transit circles past and present', *The Observatory* **69** (1949); 141-2.

H. Minow, *Historisches Vermessungs Instrumente* [Historical Surveying instruments in museum collections], (Wiesbaden, 1982, 2nd edition 1990).

J. A. Repsold, Zur Geschichte der astronomischen Messwerkzeug, vol 1, 1430-1830, (Leipzig, 1908) and vol 2, 1830-1900, (Leipzig, 1914).

A. W. Skempton and J. Brown, 'John and Edward Troughton' *NRRS* **27** (1973); 233-262.

P. Stroobant, *Les Observatoires et les Astronomes,* (Observatoire Royale de Belgique, Brussels, 1907). [World list of observatories and their equipment].

P. Stroobant, *Les Observatoires Magnetiques,* (Observatoire Royale de Belgique, Brussels, 1910). [World list of magnetic observatories and their equipment].

A. N. Stimson, 'Some Board of Longitude instruments in the nineteenth century', in P. R. de Clerq (editor) *Nineteenth Century Scientific Instruments and Their Makers,* (Leiden and Amsterdam, 1985).

R. G. W. Anderson, J. Burnett and B. Gee, *Handlist of Scientific Instrument-Makers' Trade Catalogues, 1600-1914,* (National Museums of Scotland Information Series No. 8), (Edinburgh, 1990) lists 20 Cooke, 1 Troughton and 14 Troughton & Simms catalogues, with their locations.

The VI archive holds catalogues of Cooke, Troughton & Simms, and Vickers Instruments products, books by H. D. Taylor, E. W. Taylor, and others associated with the firm in recent years, as well as post-war publicity films. The Science Museum Library Trade Literature Collection has some leaflets and catalogues post-dating those listed in Anderson et al.

# Index

ABERDEEN City, 14
Adams, Dudley, 24
Adie
  John and Patrick, 27
  Patrick, rangefinder, 47
Advertising, 7, 28, 42, 48, *53*, 61, *82*
Airy, [Sir] George Biddell (1801-92), 31, 32, 34-40, 42-3, 45, 51
Albert, Prince Consort
  Telescope, 52
Aldis, 75
Altazimuth circle
  Chapultepec, T. & S., 43
  Edinburgh, T. & S., 26-7
  'Lee' circle, Troughton's, 11, *15*
  Palermo, Ramsden's, 8-9
  Pearson's, Troughton's, 26
  Pond's, Troughton's, 16
  Troughton's prices, 14
  von Brühl's, Troughton's, 11
  Greenwich, T. & S., 38, *38*
Aluminium-bronze, 4, 41, 56
American Philosophical Society, 19-20
Argo Company, 73-5
Astronomical Dining Club – see Royal
Astronomical photography, 61, 66-8, 70
Astronomical Society – see Royal

BAILY, Francis (1774-1844), 28, 36
Baker, C. (Holborn) Ltd, 93
Baker, Captain T. Y., 81-2
Balances, 14, 19
Bardin, William (c1740-98), 12
Barker, Francis Henry (1865-1922), 76
Barometer
  Troughton's, 20, 28
  T. & S., 35
Barrow, Henry (1790-1870), 16
Beck, Joseph (c1829-91), 32
Berge, John, 13
Berger, C. L., 58

Bird, John (1709-1776), 37
Board of Longitude, 4, 10, 22
Board of Ordnance, 10, 22, 27, 32, 36
Boys, Professor [Sir] Charles Vernon (1855-1944), 82
Bridges-Lees, J., 65
British Antarctic Expedition, theodolites, 69, *71*
British Association for the Advancement of Science
  Ipswich Meeting, 38
  York Meeting, 50, 84
'British Circle', Troughton's, 11
British Optical Manufacturers' Association, 75
British Separators, 79
Brockbank, J. & S., 12
Buckingham Works – see Cooke premises
Buff, G. L., 58

CAILLARD, G. S. E., 76
Casella (Electronics) Ltd, 93
Casella, C. F. & Co, 80
Casella, L. P., 97
Cauchoix, Robert Aglaé (1776-1845), 29, 34
Charlton Works – see Troughton & Simms
Cheshire, R. W., 81
Christie, W. H. M. (1845-1922), 34
Christie, [Sir] William H. M. (1845-1922), 45, 47, 59
City & Guilds Institute, instruments for, 45
Clock pendulums, Troughton's, 20
Clockmakers' Company, 19
Colby, [Sir] Thomas (1784-1852), 22, 27
Cole family
  Benjamin (junior) (1725-1813), 6-7, 14
  Benjamin (senior) (1695-1766), 6
Comparator of length, Cooke's, for van den Kerchove, 62
Connell, W. H., 83-4
Cooke family, *49, 51*
  Barnard (1812-87), 51
  Charles Frederick ('Fred') (1836-98), 52, *52, 54,* 57-8, 65-6
  Hannah (1812-84), 50, 57, 65
  Thomas (1807-68), 36, 41, 44, 46, *52*
  Thomas (1839-1919), 38, *52*

Cooke instruments etc – see also Equatorials
    Dividing engine, 54-6, 82, 99, *99*
    Domes, 45, 58-60, *60, 61, 72*
    Drainage level, 51, 69
    Transit, for India, *55*, 56
Cooke patents, 65
Cooke photographic lens, 66, 73, *73*, 89-90
Cooke premises
    Buckingham Works, York, 51-4, *54*, 56-7, *58*, 62, *63-4*, 69,
        74-5, *75-7*, 79, 90
    Cape Town, 63, 79, 90
    Coney Street, York, 51
    Fort Winnipeg, 69
    Johannesburg, 63, 90
    Salisbury, 90
    Southampton Street, Strand, 52, *55*
    Stag Place, London, 94
    Toronto, Montreal and Edmonton, 90
    Victoria Street, London, 64
Cooke, T. & Sons, 48, 65 – see also flow diagram
Cooke, Troughton & Simms, 78
Cooke, Troughton & Simms, S. Africa (Pty) Ltd, 90
Cooke, Troughton & Simms Inc., 90
Cooke, Troughton & Simms Ltd, 80, 93
Cooke, Troughton & Simms premises
    Broadway, Westminster, 79, *79*
    'Kingsway North', York, 87
    Haxby Road, York, 86, *86*, 90
Curties, Michael, 93
Cushing, Thomas, 65

DALLOWAY, Joseph, 12
Dawson, [Sir] Trevor (1866-1931), 80
Denholm Fraser, H. A., magnetometer, 69, *70*
Dividing, 2, 19, 25, 32, 80, 85
Dividing engine
    Cooke's, 54-6, 82, 99, *99*
    East India Company order, 37
    Hassler's, 32, 98
    Simms', 32, 99
    Troughton's, 6, 8, *9*, 47, 98-9
Dollond, 12, 17, 21, 38
Domes – see Cooke
Donkin, Bryan (1768-1855), 17, 21, 29-30, 32, 36
Donkin, Bryan (junior), 21, 36
Drechsler, Georg and son, 12
Drummond, Thomas (1797-1840), 22, 27
Dyson, J., 92

EAST India Company, 10, 22, 28, 32, 35, 37-8, 54
Edinburgh Astronomical Institution, 26, 27
Elliot Bros., 74
Elliptograph, T. & S., 38
Elphinstone, [Sir] Keith (1865-1941), 74
Equatorials by Cooke, *27, 49, 64, 68*
    Cadiz, 60
    Copenhagen, 60
    For Japan, sold to W. T. Henley, 61
    Franklin-Adams, 66, *67*
    Glasgow, 60
    Liège University, 60
    Madras, 60
    Newall's, 53, 57, *57*
    Poona, 60
    Rio de Janeiro, 60-1, *72*
    Scarborough (Wigglesworth), 59
    Sydney, 60
    Trieste (Pola), 60
    Uccle, 60
Equatorials by Troughton
    Armagh, 10, *10*, 17
    Coimbra, 9
    Huddart's, *17*, 29
    South's, 22, 28-9, *30*, 32, 34
Equatorials by Troughton & Simms, *27*
    Harvard, Tuscaloosa and West Point, 37
    'Northumberland', 37
    Brussels, 37
    Liverpool, 37
Evans, Rev. Lewis (1755-1827), 1
Everest, [Sir] George (1790-1866), 16, 27-9, 35
    'Everest' theodolite, 28, *39, 94*
Exchequer Standards, 14
Exhibitions, Fairs and Shows
    British Empire, 1924, 79
    British Industries, Birmingham 1935, 86
    British Industries, Buenos Aires 1931, 84, *84*
    London 1851, 38
    London 1862, 41, 44, *49*, 51-4
    London 1871, 61, 64
    Paris 1855, 51
    Vienna 1873, 61
    Yorkshire 1857 and 1866, 51-2

FAYRER family
    James, 13, 15-16, 29, 31
    James (junior), 16

Fereday-Palmer Stress Recorder, 82
Fergusson, James, 65
    Percentage theodolite, 69
Fibercheck, 95
Fleet Street, *12*, 78, *33*
    No. 136, 6, *20*
    No. 138, *20*, 33, 41-2, 78
Fletcher, Isaac (1827-79), 50
Folque, General Felipe, 35
Fontana, Felice, 15
Forbes, George (1849-1936), 47
Forth Bridge survey, 58, *59*
    Theodolite, Cooke's, 58, *97*
Franklin-Adams, John (1843-1912), 66-8, *67*
Frodsham, Charles, 51

GILBERT, William, 12, 22, 35
Gill, [Sir] David (1843-1914), 60
Gold-palladium alloy, 17
Gravatt, William, 50-1
Gray, William, 50-1
Great Trigonometrical Survey of India – see Survey
Grenfell, H. H. (1845-1906)
    Grenfell gunsight, 65
Greville, Hon. Charles (1749-1809), 11
Groombridge, Stephen (1755-1832), 11, *31*
Grubb, Thomas & Co (Grubb, Parsons), 45, 53, 59, 85
Guinand, Pierre, 40

HALLIMOND, A. F., 92
Hassler, Ferdinand (1770-1843), *19*, 19-20, 32, 34, 98
Heape-Grylls camera, 82
Heath, Thomas (1698-1773), 6
Henley, W. T., 61
Herschel, J. F. W. (1792-1871), 28
Hilger, Adam Ltd, 61, 75-7, 80
Hodgson, J. A.
    Transit theodolite, 35
Horizon, glass, Troughton's, 20
Huddart, James (1741-1816), 29, *17*

INSTITUTION of Civil Engineers, 32

JEFFCOTT tacheometer, 77, 84
Jones, Thomas (1775-1852), 24, 26

LAWRENCE, Robert, 16
Lee, Dr John (1783-1866), *15*, 11

Leitz, 89
Lens, *3*
    Achromatic, 2, *3*
    'Cooke', 70
    Grinding, 40, 53, *90*
Levels, *95*
    Bolton's, 65, 69
    Cooke's drainage, 51, 69
    Cooke's self-checking, 83
    Cushing's, 65
    Engineers', 84
    Gravatt's, 28
    Troughton's, 20
Linn, John, 80
London Mechanics Institution, 25-6
Loomis, Elias, 35
Lowe, Gavin (c1743-1815), 11, *15*

MACCA baseline apparatus, 85-6
Magnetometer, Cooke's, 69, *70*
Makdougall Brisbane, Sir Thomas (1773-1860), 17, 99
Marindin, Arthur Henry (1868-1947), 47
Maskelyne, Nevil (1732-1811), (Astronomer Royal), 16
Maudslay; Maudslay & Field, 32, 36-7
May, Charles, 38
McArthur, J.; McArthur Microscopes Ltd, 92-3, *92*
McCaw, G. T., 85
Meek, Sir James (1815-91), 57
Merz, 39-40
Microscope
    Bench, 84, 87, *88*
    Interference, 93
    McArthur, 91-2, *92*
    Petrological, 89
    Phase-contrast, 93
    Vickers Projection, *83*, 84, 86-7, 91, *96*
Mining instruments, Cooke's, 77
Montojo, Don Saturnino, 35
Mudge, William (1762-1820), 22
Mural circle
    Brussels, 37
    Calton Hill, Edinburgh, 26-7, 32
    Cambridge, 37, 42
    Greenwich (Troughton's), 16-9, *18*, 96, Back cover
    Harvard, USA, 37
    Lucknow, 37
    Trivandrum, 37
    West Point, 37

NAUTICAL top, Troughton's, 20
Newall, Hugh Frank (1857-1944), 57
Newall, Robert Stirling (1812-89), 53-4, 57
Northumberland telescope, 34
Norton, (cabinet maker), 29
Nutting, John, 26, 32

OBSERVATORY
    Adelaide, 60
    Armagh, 10, 17
    Brussels, 37
    Cadiz, 35, 60
    Calton Hill, Edinburgh, 26-7
    Cambridge, 34, 37, 43
    Cape of Good Hope, 15, 51, 60, *60*, 85
    Chapultepec, 43
    Coimbra University, 9, 10
    Copenhagen, 60
    Dorpat, 14
    East India Company, Madras, 10
    East India Company, Lambeth, 41
    Fleet Street, 9
    Georgetown, Washington, 37
    Glasgow, 60
    Gotha, 14
    Greek National, 57
    Greenwich, 24, 25, 42, *61*
    Greenwich Royal, 32, 35, 38, 59
    Harvard, 37, 43
    Leipzig, 14
    Liège University, 60
    Liverpool, 37
    Lucknow, 37
    Madras, 60
    Melbourne, 37
    Odessa, 60
    Palermo, 8-9, 16-17
    Pola, 47
    Poona, 60
    Radcliffe, Oxford, 37
    Rio de Janeiro, 60, 69-70, *72*
    Simms', at No. 138 Fleet Street, 34
    Simms', Carshalton, 34
    Sir James South's, 26, 29
    Sofia, 60
    St Petersburg, 14, 26
    Sydney, 60
    Tacubaya, 43
    Teramo, 60
    Trieste (Pola), 60
    Trivandrum, Madras, 37
    Troughton's, at No. 136 Fleet Street, 11-2
    Tuscaloosa, 37
    Uccle, 60
    Washington Naval, 45
    West Point, USA, 37
Optical Comparator, Cooke's, 86
Optical Convention, 1926, 82
Optical Dividing Head, Cooke's, 87
Optical glass, 5, 40, 83
Optical munitions, 47, 64, 86-7, 90, 95
Ordnance Survey, 35

PANTOGRAPH, Cooke's, 63
Pattinson, Hugh (1796-1858), 50
Pearson, William (1767-1847), 26
Peterborough Court, 7, *12, 20*, 22, 32-4, 42
Phillips, John (1800-74), 50
Pictet, Marc-Auguste (1752-1825), 15
Pillar construction, 3, 10
Platinum, 4, 17, 18-9, 36
Pneumatic despatch system, Cooke's, 61, 65, 79
Pollen, Arthur Joseph Hungerford (1866-1937), 73-5
        Aim-Correction System, 73-5
        Rangefinder, 74-5, *74*
Pond, John (1767-1836), (Astronomer Royal), 16, 24

QUAESTOR, Vickers Instruments, 95-6

RAILWAY surveys, 35
Ramsden, Jesse (1735-1800), 6, 8, 11, 13
        Theodolite, 19, 22, 27, 35
Rangefinder
        Cooke's Admiralty, 73-4
        Cooke-Pollen, 74-5
        Waymouth, 74
        Waymouth-Cooke, 82
        Marindin, 47
        Pollen's, 74-5
Ransomes & May, 38
Rehe, Samuel, 13
Reichenbach, 43
Rodolite, Cooke's, 92
Ross, (Sir) John (1777-1856), 20

Rowley, John (c1668-1728), 6
Roy, William (1726-1790), 11, 22
Royal Astronomical Dining Club, 19, 34
Royal Astronomical Society, 11, 15, 29, 34, 36, 52
Royal Military Academy, 35, 44
Royal Navy, 10, 44, 47
Royal Society, 14, 19, 21, 29, 39
Royal Society of Arts, 24
Royal Society of Edinburgh, 19

Scott Maxwell, Peter D., 90
Sector, Troughton & Simms, 1831, 22
Sextants, 10-11, 14, 18, 47
Sheepshanks, Richard (1794-1855), 30, 34, 36-7, 99
Shuckburgh-Evelyn, Sir George (1751-1804), 14
Simms family, *25*
    Alfred Septimus, 24-5
    Arthur Davison (1891-1976), 78, 80, 91, *91*
    Frederick Walter (1803-65), 24, *25*, 26, 35
    George (1799-1886), James (1792-), John (1798-1879), 24
    Henry (1800-71), 25, 32
    James (1828-1915), 33, *34*, 40-7
    James (1862-1939), *41*, 47-8, 77
    William (1763-1791), 24
    William (1793-1860), *26*, 24-40
    William (1817-1907), *26*, 35-6, 41, 44
    William (1860-1938), *41*, 47-8, 77
    William Henry (1820-), 32
Simms Wilson, James (1893-1976), 78, 91-2, *91*
Smith, Francis, 93, *93*
Smith, R. L., 84
Smyth, Charles Piazzi (1819-1900), 43, 61
Society of Civil Engineers, 13, 19
South African gold fields surveys, 63
South, Sir James (1785-1867), 11, 26, 28-9, *30*, 32, 34
Spence, Graeme, 12
Spencer Jones, [Sir] Harold, (Astronomer Royal), 84-5
St Bride's parish
    Lease of No. 138 to Simms, 34
    School, 30
    Simms' family duties, 33
Standards of length, 14, 36, 98
    'Euphrates Expedition', 36
    'Imperial Standard', 37
    10 foot Ordnance bar, 36
    Baily's, 36
    Board of Ordnance, 15

British, 32
Cape of Good Hope Observatory, 36
Danish Government, 15
Imperial, 38
Metric, 44
Public, in London, 44, *44*, 98
Royal Astronomical Society, 15, 36
Schumacher's, 36
Struve's, 36
Survey of Ireland, 27
Station pointer, 12, 47
Steam carriage, Cooke's, 52
Steam engine, Cooke's, 51
Strange, Lt-Col Alexander (1818-76), 40, 44, 63
Suddard, Jane, Nancy and Thomas, 7, 13
Survey of India, 41, *41*, 44, *70*
    Cooke levels, 57
    Instruments for, 28, 35
Survey of Ireland, 27
    Instruments for, 20
Surveying instruments, 11

Tavistock, conference, 80
    Theodolite, 80-2, *81*, 84
Taxes and Duties
    Optical glass, 4, 40
    Window, 4
Taylor, Alfred (1863-1940), 65, *65*
Taylor, Edward Wilfred (1891-1980), 77, 80-2, 84-5, *85*, 87, 89, 91
Taylor, Harold Dennis (1862-1943), 65, *71*, 76, 85, 89
    Awards, 68, 71
    Photo-visual objective, 66
    Publications, 66, 70
    Triple apochromatic lens, 66
Taylor, Taylor & Hobson, 66, *73*, 75, 77, 89-90
Tellurometer, 92, *92*, 94
Theodolites, *39*, *71*
    Cooke's 'War Department', 61, 64
    Cooke's, 51, 55
    'Everest', 28, *39*, *94*
    Tavistock, 80-2, *81*, 84
Thomas Wright (c1693-1764), 6
Toolroom Microscope, C. T. & S., 87
Trade Fairs – see Exhibitions
Transit circles, by T. & S., *31*, *47*
    Cambridge, 43
    Georgetown, 37

Harvard, 43
Tacubaya, 43
Tuscaloosa, 37
Greenwich, *44*
By C. T. & S:, Greenwich, 85
Transit of Venus Expeditions, 45, *46*
Transit telescope
  Cooke's, 56, 84, *55*
  Troughton's, 21, *23*, 26
Troughton family, 7
  Edward (c1753-1835), 8-34, *16*, 38
  John (1716-88), 6, *8*, 13, 22
  John (1739-1807), 6-8, 10-13, 22
Troughton instruments – see also Altazimuth, Equatorial and
  Transit
  Barometer, 5, 20, 28
  Beam compass, 14, *15*
  Circles, 9, 11, 14, *15*, 16-20, *21*, 24, 38, *98*
  Dip sector, 28
  Dividing engine, *9*
  Geodetic pendulum, 29
  Level and staff, 28
  Orrery, *11*
  Portable transit, 28
  Protractor, *8*
  Quadrant, *9*, 10
  Reflecting circle, 11
  Theodolites, 10, 35
  Zenith sector, 21
Troughton, J. & E., 7, 10, 12-3, 97
Troughton & Simms, 26-8, 30, 35, 38, 40, 42-8, 54, 58, 69, 97
  24-inch theodolites, 26
  3-ft theodolite, for Strange, 32
  Advertising, 28, 42, 48
  Altazimuth, Greenwich, 38, *38*
  Barometer, 35
  Charlton Works, 42, *42*, 45, *45*, 47-8, *47*, *48*, 89
  Equatorial, Greenwich, 38
  Price-list, 21
  Repairs at Greenwich, 38, 45
  Theodolites, 27-8, 34-5, 39, 41
  Transit circle, Greenwich, 38

'Water telescope', *43*
  Zenith instruments, 38, *41*
Tulley, Charles (1782-1846), 12
Turret clock, Cooke's, 51-2, *56*
Twyman, Frank (1876-1959), 76, 80

UNIFILAR magnetometer, Cooke's, 69
Universal milling and shaping machine, Cookes', 82

VALLÉ, H. W., 58
Van Hoesen & Wilson bubble-grinding machine, 65
Vickers Ltd, etc, 58, 64-5, 72-3, 75-80, 90-1
Vickers Contour Projection Apparatus, 86
Vickers Hardness Testing Machine, 82
Vickers Instruments, 93
Vickers Instruments Ltd, 94
Vickers Projection Microscope, *83*, 84, 86-7, 91, *96*
Von Brühl, Count H. M., 11

WADLEY, T. L., 92
Watkin, Major H. S. S. (1843-1905)
  Mekometer, 64-5, *65*
  Artillery Position Finder, 64-5
  Depression rangefinder, *78*
Watts, E. R. & Sons, 80, 83
Waugh, Andrew Scott (1810-78), 35
Wehlisch, Richard (c1818-1904), 55
Wigglesworth, James (1825-88), 57, 59
Wigglesworth, Robert, 57, 59
Wild, Heinrich, 80, 83, 85
Wilkes, Charles, USN, 34
Winterhalter, Lt A. J., USN, 45, 47
Wollaston, W. H. (1766-1826), 18
Wollaston's dip sector, 12
World War I, 47, 75-7
World War II, 86-7

YEATES, Andrew (1800-1866), 16
Yolland, William, 27

ZEISS, 80, 83, 86, 88
Ziegler and Hager's tacheograph, 65